Introduction

Welcome to your personal journey toward making one of the most significant decisions of your life: choosing the right college and setting meaningful goals for your future. This guided notebook is crafted especially for you—whether you're a high school senior, taking a gap year, or already navigating the college experience. Our aim is to help you make informed decisions and set a strong foundation for your academic and personal growth.

Purpose of This Notebook

The transition into college is an exciting time filled with possibilities, but it can also be overwhelming. With countless options and factors to consider, it's easy to feel unsure about the path ahead. This notebook is designed to:

- Encourage Reflection: Thought-provoking prompts will help you identify your passions, strengths, and aspirations.
- Provide Practical Advice: Each chapter offers insights on key considerations like academic programs, campus culture, financial planning, and career opportunities.
- Offer Reassurance: Affirmations remind you that it's okay to feel uncertain and that you're not alone in this journey.

How To Use This Notebook

Each section is thoughtfully organized to guide you through different aspects of the decision-making and goal-setting process:

- Reflective Exercises: Engage with activities that prompt you to think deeply about what you want from your college experience.
- Actionable Tips: Gain practical advice on navigating applications, scholarships, and adjusting to college life.
- Goal-Setting Frameworks: Learn how to set SMART (Specific, Measurable, Achievable, Relevant, Time-bound) goals to keep you focused and motivated.

Feel free to move at your own pace. This is your journey, and it's important that it reflects your unique needs and timeline.

Additional Resources are listed at the end of this guide (starting on page 101).

The Power of Collaboration

While this notebook is a personal tool, collaborating with others can enrich your experience:

- Mentors: Seek guidance from teachers, counselors, or professionals who can offer valuable insights.
- Parents and Guardians: Involve your family in discussions; they can provide support and may highlight considerations you haven't thought of.
- Friends: Share your thoughts and plans with peers who are going through similar experiences.

Open conversations can lead to new perspectives and help solidify your decisions.

Embrace the Journey

Remember, choosing a college and setting goals is not just about the destination but also about the journey of self-discovery. Be patient with yourself, stay open-minded, and trust that each step you take brings you closer to where you're meant to be.

We're excited to accompany you on this path toward a fulfilling college experience and beyond. Let's get started!

Section I

Choosing a college is more than just selecting a place to study—it's about finding an environment where you can thrive academically, socially, and personally. This first section invites you to embark on a series of thought exercises designed to clarify your preferences and priorities. By reflecting on what truly matters to you, you'll be better equipped to identify colleges that align with your goals and values.

In the upcoming chapters, you'll delve into questions about your academic interests, desired campus culture, ideal location, and financial considerations. These exercises will help you uncover insights about yourself and what you're seeking in a college experience.

As you work through this section, remember that honesty with yourself is key. Take the time to ponder each question deeply, and don't hesitate to jot down any thoughts or feelings that arise. Engaging in open conversations with mentors, parents, or friends can also provide additional perspectives to enrich your decision-making process.

01 Understanding Your Finanical Priorities

02 Exploring Academic Programs and Majors

03 Understanding the Social Scene

04 Navigating Dorm Life and Housing Options

05 College Admission Requirements

06 Exploring College Campuses Through Visits

Let's begin this **journey of self-discovery** to find the college that's the perfect fit for you.

Chapter 1: Understanding Your Financial Priorities

Balancing the allure of a prestigious institution with the practicality of graduating debt-free is a challenge many students face. This chapter will help you explore your financial priorities, understand different funding options, and plan accordingly.

Whether you're considering taking out loans or aiming to minimize debt, this section provides the tools and insights to make informed decisions.

PRESTIGE VS. AFFORDABILITY

One of the first considerations is determining what matters most to you: attending a prestigious school that may offer enhanced career prospects or focusing on affordability to reduce or eliminate student debt.

FACTORS TO CONSIDER

- **Career Goals**: Does your chosen field place significant emphasis on the reputation of the institution?
- **Return on Investment (ROI)**: Will the potential benefits of a prestigious degree outweigh the costs in the long run?
- **Personal Circumstances**: How will debt impact your lifestyle and choices after graduation?

REFLECTION EXERCISES

PRIORITIES

What are some of your top priorities when choosing a college?

- [ ] Prestige
- [ ] Cost
- [ ] Location
- [ ] Academic Rigor
- [ ] Accommodations
- [ ] Campus Atmosphere
- [ ] Major Options

- [ ] Quality of Professors
- [ ] Minor/Certificate Options
- [ ] _____________
- [ ] _____________
- [ ] _____________
- [ ] _____________

HOW COMFORTABLE ARE YOU TAKING ON DEBT?

____

____

____

____

____

____

____

PRESTIGE VS AFFORDABILITY

Can you find a balance between prestige and affordability that suits your goals? Use this scale to visualize where your thoughts lie between prestige and cost.

Use the pre-marked needles or draw your own.

Understanding Student Loans

If you're considering loans to finance your education, it's essential to understand the types available and their implications.

 FEDERAL LOANS

- **Direct Subsidized Loans**: For undergraduates with demonstrated financial need. The government pays the interest while you're in school at least half-time.
- **Direct Unsubsidized Loans**: Available to undergraduates and graduate students; not based on financial need. Interest accrues while you're in school.
- **Direct PLUS Loans**: For graduate students or parents of undergraduates to cover education expenses not met by other financial aid.

PRIVATE LOANS

- **Offered by Banks and Credit Unions**: May require a credit check or co-signer. Interest rates can be variable and higher than federal loans.
- **Less Flexible Repayment Options**: Fewer protections like deferment or income-driven repayment plans.

Comparing Private and Federal Loans		
Feature	**Federal Loans**	**Private Loans**
Credit Check Required	No (except PLUS loans)	Yes
Interest Rates	Fixed, often lower	Fixed or variable, may be higher
Repayment Options	Flexible, income-driven	Less Flexible
Forgiveness Programs	Available for certain careers	Not typically offered
Borrowing Limits	Pre-set limits	Variable

Additional Resources: Bank and lender websites, studentaid.gov, college financial aid offices, high school counselors

REFLECTION EXERCISES

Are you willing to take on private loans, or would you prefer to rely solely on federal aid? Mark your thoughts on the line below.

Federal Loans |————————— Mix —————————| Private Loans

How will loan repayment impact your post-graduation plans and lifestyle—for example, Future traveling, budgeting for a stay-at-home parent, or are you pursuing a lucrative career to cover payments?

____

____

____

____

____

Estimating College Costs

Having a clear picture of the costs associated with each college can help you make practical decisions.

FILLING OUT THE FAFSA

The FAFSA, or Free Application for Federal Student Aid, is a form that students complete to apply for federal financial aid for college. Filling it out is important because it determines your eligibility for federal grants, loans, and work-study programs, which can significantly reduce the cost of your education. Additionally, many states and colleges use FAFSA information to award their own financial aid, so completing it maximizes your opportunities for funding your college education. Visit www.FAFSA.gov for more information. Knowing your FAFSA information will help you make accurate estimates for college costs.

FILLABLE COST ESTIMATE TABLE

Use the table below to estimate costs for each college you're considering. Many of the expenses are easy to identify, such as tuition & fees, room & board, and books & supplies. Estimates for these can often be found on college websites. Other expenses you may need to consider, depending on the college and location, are parking passes, plane tickets to visit home, or high cost of living in the area which can dramatically increase your grocery and gas costs. If you need a second copy or more space, an additional table is included on page 103.

BEFORE ADMISSIONS

College Name	Tuition & Fees	Room & Board	Books & Supplies	Other Expenses	Estimated Total Cost

TIPS FOR FILLING OUT TABLES

- **Tuition & Fees**: Check the college's official website for the most recent figures.
- **Room & Board**: Consider on-campus vs. off-campus housing costs.
- **Other Expenses**: Include transportation, personal expenses, and health insurance.

Once you receive financial aid offers from colleges you have applied to, update the table with actual figures. As a first year student, you can expect your financial aid package to arrive in late spring or early summer.*

For the net cost, subtract scholarships, grants, and loans from the total cost to find what you'll need to cover.

If you would like to use a larger version or need an extra copy, this table is also included on page 104.

College Name	Tuition & Fees	Room & Board	Books & Supplies	Other Expenses	Scholarships & Grants	Loans Offered	Net Cost

REFLECTION EXERCISES

Did anything change between your estimates and the actual costs?

____

____

____

____

Any surprising costs (either lower or higher than expected) when filling out these tables?

____

____

____

*according to: https://bigfuture.collegeboard.org

Targeting Scholarships

Scholarships can significantly reduce your financial burden. They come from various sources and often require proactive searching and application. Every dollar you save or secure through scholarships is one less you'll need to borrow. Investing time now can lead to significant financial benefits in the future.

WHERE TO LOOK FOR SCHOLARSHIPS

- **College Financial Aid Offices**: Many schools offer merit-based and need-based scholarships. Be sure to check for department scholarships as well for programs you are interested in pursuing.
- **High School Guidance Counselors**: Can provide information on local scholarships.
- **Online Scholarship Databases**: Websites like Fastweb, Scholarships.com, and the College Board Scholarship Search.
- **Community Organizations**: Local businesses, clubs, and religious organizations may offer scholarships.
- **Employers**: Some companies provide scholarships to employees or their dependents.

TIPS FOR SCHOLARSHIP APPLICATIONS

- **Start Early**: Application periods can open as early as a year before college starts.
  - Before applications are open, take time to look at various essay questions from previous years' scholarships so you can start brainstorming ideas for common essay topics.
- **Recommendation Letters:** Give your reference plenty of time and provide a summary of your achievements, grades, and a resume to assist them.
- **Stay Organized**: Keep track of deadlines and required documents.
- **Customize Applications**: Tailor your essays and responses to each scholarship's criteria. Avoid essays that are generic; check online for common examples of responses to avoid.
- **Proofread**: Ensure all application materials are free of errors. Ask a teacher, mentor, or parent to help proofread.
- **Follow Up**: Confirm receipt of your application if possible.

SCHOLARSHIP TRACKING TABLE

Organize your scholarship applications with this table. As you complete requirements, check off the associated boxes. Be sure to keep track of deadlines on your calendar so you don't miss any opportunities for **FREE** college funds. A larger version of this table is included on page 105.

Scholarship Name	Provider	Amount	Requirements	Deadline	Application Status
			☐ _______ ☐ _______ ☐ _______ ☐ _______		☹ Not Started 😐 In Progress ☺ Submitted!
			☐ _______ ☐ _______ ☐ _______ ☐ _______		☹ Not Started 😐 In Progress ☺ Submitted!
			☐ _______ ☐ _______ ☐ _______ ☐ _______		☹ Not Started 😐 In Progress ☺ Submitted!
			☐ _______ ☐ _______ ☐ _______ ☐ _______		☹ Not Started 😐 In Progress ☺ Submitted!

REFLECTION EXERCISES

What scholarships align with your achievements, background, or future goals?

____

____

____

____

How can you strengthen your scholarship applications to improve your chances of success—for example, do you have unique skills, experiences, passions, or excellent references and proofreaders?

____

____

____

____

Chapter Conclusion

Understanding your financial priorities is a crucial step in choosing the right college and setting yourself up for future success. By carefully considering the trade-offs between prestige and affordability, comprehending different loan options, estimating costs, and proactively seeking scholarships, you can make informed decisions that align with your goals and financial situation. Here are the steps you took in this chapter:

Complete the FAFSA: You will need your parents' or guardians' help with this. Filling out the FAFSA early can help secure additional federal aid.

Complete the Cost Estimates Tables: Research and fill in the estimated costs for your prospective colleges.

Research Loans: If considering loans, delve deeper into federal and private options.

Identify Scholarships: Use the tracking table to list scholarships you're eligible for and start the application process.

It's always a good idea to discuss your research and thoughts with a trusted mentor, parent, and/or friend.

EMBRACE THE JOURNEY

Financial planning may seem daunting, but it's a powerful step toward achieving your educational and career aspirations. Stay focused, organized, and proactive, and you'll navigate this challenge successfully.

Chapter 2: Exploring Academic Programs and Majors

ACADEMICS IS USUALLY THE FIRST THING STUDENTS THINK ABOUT WHEN THEY START THINKING ABOUT COLLEGE.

While college is much more than classes and continuing education, a major goal of college is to deliver the necessary skills and knowledge to be able to start a successful career. Selecting a major is a significant step in your college journey, but keep in mind it's also one that many students revisit along the way.

This chapter is designed to help you explore your interests, understand how they translate into potential careers, and identify colleges that offer strong programs in your areas of interest. We'll also discuss the flexibility of academic paths, including the option of minors and certificates, to ensure you're set up for success even if your goals evolve.

SELF ASSESSMENT EXCERCISES

⊘ **LIST ACTIVITIES OR SUBJECTS THAT EXCITE YOU**

____

____

____

⊘ **LIST HOBBIES OR TOPICS YOU ENJOY LEARNING ABOUT**

____

____

____

⊘ **IDENTIFY SUBJECTS WHERE YOU EXCEL ACADEMICALLY**

____

____

⊘ **ASK MENTORS OR TEACHERS WHAT SKILL OR TALENTS THEY SEE YOU EXCEL AT**

____

____

Exploring Your Interests

Understanding what genuinely interests you is the foundation of choosing the right major.

There are many available resources for diving further into your interests or personality and tying that to potential careers. Some of the resources below are free while others require a fee.

- **Online Quizzes**: Take free online assessments to discover careers that match your interests - the career cluster quiz found at http://www.educationplanner.org/students/ is one example.
- **Skill Matching Tools**: Input your skills into platforms that suggest compatible careers.
- **Interest Inventories**: Use tools that align your hobbies and preferences with potential job paths.
- **Myers-Briggs Type Indicator (MBTI)**: Offers insights into your personality and potential career fits. Test is available at MBTIonline.com for a fee.
- **Strong Interest Inventory**: Matches your interests with possible careers for a fee.

High school counselors may be able to provide access to these or other similar tools with free access for students. Reach out to you counselor to find what your school offers.

REFLECTION EXERCISES

What subjects or activities make you lose track of time?

____

____

Which classes have you enjoyed the most, and why?

____

____

What challenges have you overcome, and what skills did you use?

____

____

Connecting Interests to Careers

Once you've identified your interests and strengths, the next step is to see how they align with potential careers.

RESEARCHING POTENTIAL CAREERS

Getting out into the world and exploring potential careers first hand or through the insight of those in the field is a great way to gain insight.

- **Job Shadowing**: Spend a day with a professional in a field you're interested in.
- **Informational Interviews**: Talk to individuals working in careers you find appealing.
- **Internships and Volunteer Work**: Gain hands-on experience to test your interest in a field.
- **School or Community Programs**: Ask your school counselors, local library, or other community centers if there are any field trips, guided tours, or seminars available.

If you would rather look into potential careers on your own, here are a few ideas for doing that.

- **Career Websites**: Utilize resources like the Bureau of Labor Statistics' Occupational Outlook Handbook or O*NET Online to explore different careers.
- **Professional Associations**: Explore websites of professional organizations related to your fields of interest.
- **Industry Publications**: Subscribe to magazines or journals in fields that interest you.
- **Blogs and Podcasts**: Follow industry experts and read articles or listen to episodes about trends and opportunities.
- **Videos and Virtual Tours**: Watch videos where professionals discuss their careers or view virtual tours of facilities and workplaces.
- **Webinars and Online Panels**: Attend virtual events focused on career exploration.

UNDERSTANDING JOB OUTLOOKS AND REQUIREMENTS

As you identify a few careers that interest you, make sure to think about these questions:

- **Educational Requirements**: What degrees or certifications are necessary?
- **Job Growth Projections**: Are opportunities in the field expanding?
- **Salary Expectations**: Does the potential income align with your financial goals?

Whether you participate in in-person or online career exploration, take notes so you can remember and reflect on what you learned later.

____

____

____

____

REFLECTION EXERCISES

Which careers align with your top interests and strengths?

____

____

____

What are the pros and cons of these career paths?

____

____

____

How do these careers fit with your long-term goals?

____

____

____

____

FINDING COLLEGES THAT SUPPORT YOUR CAREER ASPIRATIONS

After narrowing down potential majors and careers, it's time to find colleges that offer strong programs in those areas. Use the note sections to keep track of what you're learning and thinking.

RESEARCHING COLLEGES

- **Program Strength**: Look for colleges known for excellence in your field of interest.
- **Faculty Expertise**: Research professors and their work to gauge the department's quality.
- **Facilities and Resources**: Consider the availability of labs, studios, libraries, and equipment.

UTILIZING COLLEGE SEARCH TOOLS

- **College Board's BigFuture**: Filter schools based on majors offered.
- **Peterson's College Search**: Find detailed information on programs and admissions.
- **University Websites**: Explore departmental pages for curricula and faculty profiles.
- **Comparison Websites**: Services like College Scorecard can help compare programs and outcomes between colleges

CAMPUS VISITS AND VIRTUAL TOURS

- **Attend Open Houses**: Talk to faculty and current students about the programs.
- **Sit in on Classes**: Get a feel for teaching styles and course content.
- **Explore Online Content**: Many colleges offer virtual tours and webinars.
- **College Visit Checklist**: Use the checklist in Chapter 6 to optimize your visits.

Expanding Your Horizons **Beyond** Traditional Careers

While assessments and general career or major information can offer guidance, it's important to remember that they are just starting points. The world of careers is vast, and many opportunities exist beyond traditional roles associated with a particular major. As you dive into a major, you will discover so many other opportunities for a career after college that you maybe didn't know were available or would not have connected to a particular major. Don't get too bogged down in narrowing down a very specific post-college career. A policy professor recently told me that the most common career for his graduates was anything except policy; the skills learned in college can be applicable to many careers. The important thing at this point is to be thinking of your interests and passions and connecting that to a major.

Examples of unexpected careers for certain majors:

Geology Majors often find careers in mining or oil industries. However, many other opportunities exist for geology majors, including:
- *Forensic Investigator*: Applying geological knowledge to solve crimes.
- *Researcher*: Conducting studies on climate change or natural resources.
- *Agricultural Adviser*: Helping improve soil health and farming practices.
- *Writer*: Communicating scientific information to the public through articles or books.
- *Policy Advisor*: Shaping environmental policies at governmental or NGO levels.

Education Majors traditionally work in classrooms in private or public schools. However, many other career paths exist:
- *Entrepreneur:* Starting a micro-school or educational startup.
- *International Educator*: Teaching in different countries and experiencing new cultures.
- *Curriculum Expert*: Designing educational materials and programs.
- *Educational Consultant*: Advising schools or districts on best practices.
- *Instructional Coach*: Mentoring other teachers to enhance their teaching strategies.

Embracing Flexibility and Change

It's important to recognize that changing majors is common. Studies show that an average of 30% of students change their major at least once before graduating, and the percentage can be much higher in certain fields.* Don't stress too much about knowing exactly what you want to do for the rest of your life. Have a general idea, and allow yourself to work through the details as you live new experiences and gain more knowledge (and wisdom!) along the way.

PREPARING FOR POTENTIAL CHANGES

- **Choose a College with Diverse Strengths**: If you're undecided or considering multiple fields, select a school that excels in several areas.
- **Understand Core Curriculum Requirements**: Some colleges have flexible general education requirements that allow you to explore different disciplines.
- **Stay Open-Minded**: Allow yourself the freedom to discover new interests.

STRATEGIES FOR SUCCESS DESPITE CHANGES

- **Academic Advising**: Regularly meet with advisors to discuss your interests and degree requirements.
- **Transferable Skills**: Focus on developing skills like communication, critical thinking, and problem-solving that are valuable in any field.
- **Plan Ahead**: Be aware of prerequisites for potential majors to keep your options open.

REFLECTION EXERCISES

How comfortable are you with the possibility of changing your major?

____

____

What steps can you take to ensure a smooth transition if you decide to switch fields?

____

____

____

*National Center for Educational Statistics

Considering Minors and Certificates

Minors and certificates offer opportunities to broaden your knowledge and skill set beyond your major. A minor might also be an option if you switch majors - those classes you took for a major you're no longer interested in may allow you to earn a minor.

BENEFITS OF MINORS AND CERTIFICATES

- **Complement Your Major**: Enhance your primary field of study with additional expertise.
- **Pursue Personal Interests**: Study a subject you're passionate about without committing to a full major.
- **Increase Marketability**: Diversify your qualifications to appeal to a wider range of employers.

EXAMPLES OF COMBINING MAJORS AND MINORS

- **Major in Business with a Minor in Psychology**: Understanding human behavior can be invaluable in marketing or management.
- **Major in Biology with a Certificate in Data Analysis**: Equip yourself for fields like bioinformatics or research.
- **Major in Engineering with a Minor in Environmental Studies**: Prepare for roles in sustainable engineering practices.
- **Major in Computer Science with a Minor in Business Administration**: Gain technical expertise while understanding the business aspects to prepare for leadership roles in tech companies.
- **Major in English Literature with a Minor in Film Studies**: Combine analytical and storytelling skills to pursue careers in screenwriting, film criticism, or media production.

HOW TO EXPLORE MINORS AND CERTIFICATES

- **Review College Catalogs**: Look at available minors and certificate programs at the colleges you're considering.
- **Consult Academic Advisors**: Discuss how adding a minor or certificate fits into your academic plan.
- **Consider Workload**: Ensure you can manage the additional courses without overwhelming yourself.

Are there subjects you'd like to study in addition to your major?

____

____

____

____

____

Minors are great for studying a general topic while certificates involve a specific, applied topic of study.

Example of certificates that might be offered at colleges:

- Emergency Medical Services (EMT)
- Craft Beer Industry Professional
- Photographic Media
- Wildfire Science and Management
- User Experience (UX) Design

How might a minor or certificate enhance your career prospects?

____

____

____

____

Check out a few colleges online to see what minors or certificates are available. Do any of them strike you as interesting? If so, write them down and include what you like about them.

College	Minor/Certificate	What Interests Me
_______________	_______________	_________________________
_______________	_______________	_________________________
_______________	_______________	_________________________
_______________	_______________	_________________________
_______________	_______________	_________________________

Chapter Conclusion

Choosing a major is an important decision, but it's not set in stone. By thoroughly exploring your interests and how they connect to potential careers, you can make an informed choice that aligns with your goals. Remember that flexibility is key—many students change their majors, and that's perfectly okay. What's important is setting yourself up for success by selecting colleges that offer robust programs and support systems to accommodate your evolving interests. Stay curious, explore broadly, and allow yourself the flexibility to discover new interests as you progress through your college journey.

STEP 01

Complete Self-Assessment Exercises: Take time to reflect on your passions, strengths, and potential career paths.

STEP 02

Research Majors and Careers: Use online resources and networking to gather information.

STEP 03

Identify Suitable Colleges: Make a list of institutions that offer strong programs in your areas of interest.

STEP 04

Plan for Flexibility: Consider colleges with a variety of programs and supportive academic advising.

STEP 05

Explore Minors and Certificates: Think about additional subjects you'd like to study.

EMBRACE THE JOURNEY

Your college experience is a time of exploration and growth. Be open to new possibilities, and trust that each step you take brings you closer to discovering your true passions.

Chapter 3: Understanding the Social Scene

College life extends far beyond the classroom—it's also about the experiences, friendships, and memories you'll create along the way. The social scene plays a significant role in your overall satisfaction and personal growth during these years. This chapter will guide you through considering the extracurricular activities, campus amenities, and surrounding communities of the colleges you're evaluating. By reflecting on what social aspects are important to you, you'll be better prepared to choose a college where you can thrive both academically and personally.

EXPLORING CAMPUS ACTIVITIES

CLUBS AND ORGANIZATIONS

Most colleges offer a wide array of clubs and student organizations that cater to diverse interests.

- **Academic Clubs**: Honor societies, subject-specific groups, research opportunities.
- **Cultural Organizations**: Groups that celebrate different cultures and promote diversity.
- **Spiritual or Religious Organizations**: Groups that help you discover or keep you connected to your beliefs.
- **Special Interest Clubs**: Photography, chess, gaming, environmental activism, etc.
- **Community Service**: Volunteer groups focused on social causes.

SPORTS AND INTRAMURALS

Whether you're an athlete or enjoy casual play, sports can be a significant part of college life.

- **Varsity Sports**: Competitive teams representing the college.
- **Club Sports**: Less formal, student-run teams that compete against other schools.
- **Intramural Sports**: Recreational sports played within the college community.

ARTS AND CULTURE GROUPS

If you have a passion for the arts, consider what creative outlets are available.

- **Music**: Choirs, bands, orchestras, solo performance opportunities, guitar lessons.
- **Theater and Drama**: Acting, directing, stagecraft, improv groups.
- **Visual Arts**: Painting, sculpture, photography clubs, art galleries.
- **Writing and Journalism**: Student newspapers, literary magazines, writing workshops.

REFLECTION EXERCISES

List the types of clubs, organizations, art, or sports that interest you:

____

____

____

____

____

Research colleges you're interested in. Write down the ones that have these activities available.

____

____

____

____

____

While looking at colleges, find a few clubs, sports, artistic endeavors, or organizations that interest you that you hadn't thought of. Record the activities and colleges they're available at here:

____

____

____

____

____

____

____

____

CAMPUS FACILITIES

You've identified what organizations, sports, arts, or other activities are important to you or that you want to try during college, and which colleges you can find them at. Now it's time to consider the facilities available at each college. You may be interested in swim team and see it listed on a college website, but is the pool well kept? If you're interested in competitive sports, you might want to know what the weightlifting facility looks like or as an actor you may want to make sure your future college doesn't have just a drama department but also has a great theater to perform in. Or maybe you want a casual hobby unrelated to organized activities - like space to hike or bike.

Quality facilities can enhance your college experience by supporting your hobbies and wellness. Also consider any specialized facilities that support your interests.

- **Fitness Centers**: Gyms, weight rooms, cardio equipment.
- **Swimming Pools**: For leisure, training, or competitive swimming.
- **Sports Fields and Courts**: Soccer fields, basketball courts, tennis courts.
- **Outdoor Recreation**: Climbing walls, hiking trails, biking paths.
- **Music Practice Rooms**: For individual or group practice.
- **Art Studios**: Spaces for painting, sculpting, or other creative work.
- **Technology Labs**: Access to software, equipment, or tools for tech enthusiasts.

REFLECTION EXERCISES

What facilities will be important to you during your college years?

____

____

____

____

Be sure to add these facilities to your "must see" list for campus visits (Chapter 6)!

Evaluating the Surrounding Area

OUTDOOR ACTIVITIES

Proximity to natural environments can enrich your college experience.

- **Mountains and Ski Hills**: Opportunities for skiing, snowboarding, hiking.
- **Parks and Lakes**: Places for picnics, boating, fishing, or relaxation.
- **Trails and Nature Reserves**: For hiking, biking, bird-watching.

URBAN AMENITIES

Access to city life can provide cultural, social, and professional opportunities.

- **Shopping Centers**: Malls, boutiques, markets.
- **Entertainment**: Movie theaters, concert venues, local bands.
- **Dining**: Restaurants, cafes, diverse culinary options.
- **Cultural Institutions:** Museums, art galleries, theaters.

COMMUNITY INVOLVEMENT

Engaging with the local community can be rewarding and enriching.

- **Volunteer Opportunities**: Local nonprofits, schools, environmental projects.
- **Community Events**: Festivals, fairs, parades, farmer's markets.
- **Local Organizations:** Youth groups, civic organizations.
- **Religious Institutions**: Local churches, synagogues, temples, mosques, or other institutions.

REFLECTION EXERCISES

What local outdoor amenities are important to you?

____

What local urban amenities are important to you?

____

What community activities are you hoping to participate in?

____

Which colleges provide these opportunities? How do the colleges promote community engagement?

____

____

Prioritizing Your Social Interests

It's essential to identify which social aspects are most important to you. This will help you evaluate colleges based on how well they align with your preferences.

RANKING YOUR PRIORITIES

Use the table below to rank your social interests from most to least important. An additional copy of this table is included on page 106.

Priority Rank	Social Aspect	Notes

Instructions:

1. **List Social Aspects**: Examples include specific clubs, sports, arts, facilities, or proximity to certain amenities.
2. **Rank Them**: Place the most important aspect at rank 1, and so on.
3. **Add Notes**: Jot down any thoughts or considerations for each.
4. **Revisit**: As you learn more about available activities, revisit your rankings and adjust if needed.

Example:

Priority Rank	Social Aspect	Notes
3	Access to hiking trails	Love the outdoors; important for relaxation
1	Strong campus choir	Want to continue singing in college
2	Availability of intramural soccer	Enjoy casual sports; great for meeting people

Use the space below to jot down any additional notes, thoughts, or reflections as you consider the social scenes of different colleges.

College Name: _______________________________

____

____

____

____

College Name: _______________________________

____

____

____

____

College Name: _______________________________

____

____

____

____

Sports

Shared Interests

Music

Art

Chapter Conclusion

The social environment of a college can significantly impact your happiness and personal development during your studies. By thoughtfully considering the clubs, activities, facilities, and surrounding areas of each college, you can choose a place where you'll feel engaged and fulfilled outside the classroom. Remember that college is not only about academic growth but also about exploring your interests, building relationships, and creating lasting memories.

STEP 01

Research Campus Activities: Visit college websites to explore available clubs and organizations.

STEP 02

Connect with Current Students: Reach out to learn about their experiences.

STEP 03

Revisit Your Priorities: Adjust your rankings as you gather more information.

STEP 04

Reflect on Fit: Consider how each college aligns with your social preferences.

EMBRACE THE JOURNEY

Finding the right social environment is a personal and exciting process. Stay true to your interests and open to new experiences, and you'll find a college where you can thrive both socially and academically.

Chapter 4: Navigating Dorm Life and Housing Options

Where you live during college can greatly influence your overall experience. Housing choices affect your social life, convenience, finances, and even academic success. This chapter will guide you through evaluating the housing options available at each college you're considering. We'll explore on-campus dormitories, alternative housing, housing policies, and factors that might impact your living situation. By the end, you'll have a clearer understanding of what to expect and how to choose the best housing fit for your needs.

UNDERSTANDING HOUSING OPTIONS

ON-CAMPUS HOUSING

Most colleges offer on-campus housing, commonly known as dormitories or residence halls.

Types of Dorms
- **Traditional Dorms**: Usually consist of shared rooms with communal bathrooms.
- **Suite-Style Dorms**: Multiple bedrooms share a common living area and bathroom.
- **Apartment-Style Housing**: Include kitchens and private bathrooms, offering more independence.

Housing Policies
- **Mandatory Residency**: Some colleges require first-year students (or even all undergraduates) to live on campus.
- **Gender-Specific Housing**: Dorms may be separated by gender or offer co-ed options.
- **Specialized Housing**: Options for honors students, themed communities, or living-learning communities.

Onsite Housing Staff
Onsite housing staff can provide support, guidance, safety, community building, and conflict resolution.
- **Resident Advisors (RAs)**: Often students who live on each floor to provide support and enforce policies.
- **Housing Managers or Directors**: Professional staff overseeing residence halls.
- **Security Personnel**: Ensuring safety within dormitories.

RAs and other student housing staff may receive free or discounted housing in exchange for their responsibilities.

Is on-campus housing required at the colleges you're considering?

____

____

What type of dorm appeals to you (traditional, suite, apartment)?

____

Do you have preferences regarding gender-specific or co-ed housing?

____

Are you interested in pursuing a housing staff role for a discount?

____

OFF-CAMPUS HOUSING

Alternative housing options can provide more independence.

Options Include

- **Private Apartments**: Renting an apartment alone or with roommates.
- **Shared Houses**: Living in a house shared among several students.
- **Living at Home**: Commuting from your family home if proximity allows.

Considerations

- **Cost**: Off-campus housing may be cheaper or more expensive than dorms, depending on the area.
- **Transportation**: Commuting to campus requires considering parking, public transit, or bike routes.
- **Lease Agreements**: Typically require a longer commitment and responsibility for utilities.

REFLECTION EXERCISE

Are you interested in off-campus housing options? Why or why not?

____

____

What factors are important to you in off-campus living (cost, location independence)?

____

____

ROOMMATE SELECTION AND COMPATIBILITY

ROOMMATE ASSIGNMENT PROCESSES

If you choose off-campus housing, you will need to find your own roommate(s). Living on-campus means the college will help with this search. Some ways colleges assign roommates include:

- **Random Assignment**: Colleges may assign roommates randomly, especially for first-year students.
- **Preference Surveys**: Some schools use questionnaires about habits and preferences to match roommates.
- **Roommate Matching Systems**: Platforms where students can search for and select potential roommates.
- **Requesting Specific Roommates**: If you know someone attending the same college, you might request to room together.

FACTORS TO CONSIDER

When looking for a suitable match for a shared living space, you may want to consider:

- **Lifestyle Habits:** Sleep schedules, cleanliness, noise tolerance.
- **Personality Traits:** Introverted vs. extroverted, study habits, social preferences.
- **Values and Beliefs:** Consider if it's important to you for your roommate to share similar values.

REFLECTION EXERCISE

What factors are most important to you when selecting a roommate?

____

____

TIPS FOR A POSITIVE ROOMMATE EXPERIENCE

Having a good experience with your roommate(s) can make a big difference in your college years. Don't forget to be mindful of the type of roommate YOU are too.

- **Open Communication**: Establish expectations and boundaries early on.
- **Respect and Compromise**: Be willing to adjust and understand differing habits.
- **Seek Support When Needed**: Don't hesitate to involve housing staff, mutual friends, or other trusted advisers if issues arise.

ADDITIONAL HOUSING CONSIDERATIONS

ACCESSIBILITY AND SPECIAL NEEDS

- **Disability Accommodations**: Ensure the college can meet any physical accessibility needs.
- **Medical Requirements**: If you have medical conditions requiring special facilities or considerations.

CULTURAL OR RELIGIOUS HOUSING

- **Themed Communities**: Some colleges offer housing focused on sports, cultural, religious, or language immersion.
- **Faith-Based Housing**: Living environments that support specific religious practices.

SAFETY AND SECURITY

- **Campus Security Measures**: Keycard access, surveillance cameras, emergency protocols.
- **Neighborhood Safety**: Research the safety of surrounding areas for off-campus housing.

REFLECTION EXERCISE

Do you have any specific housing needs? If so, have you contacted the colleges' housing offices to discuss accommodations?

____

____

Are you interested in themed or faith-based housing options? If so, which colleges offer these options? Are there off-campus options that support these housing types?

____

____

What security measures are in place at the colleges you're considering? How safe are the neighborhoods near campus?

____

____

Summarizing Your Housing Priorities

It's essential to identify which social aspects are most important to you. This will help you evaluate colleges based on how well they align with your preferences.

RANKING YOUR HOUSING PREFERENCE

Use the table below to rank what's most important to you regarding housing. An additional copy of this table is available on page 106.

Priority Rank	Housing Aspect	Notes

Instructions:

1. **List Housing Aspects:** Examples include type of dorm, roommate selection, cost, location, and amenities.
2. **Rank Them:** Place the most important aspect at rank 1, and so on.
3. **Add Notes:** Include any specific details or preferences.

Example:

Priority Rank	Housing Aspect	Notes
1	Ability to choose roommate	Want to room with a friend attending same college
2	Cost	Need affordable housing options
3	Onsite housing staff	Value having RAs for support

Use the space below to jot down any additional notes, thoughts, or reflections as you consider the housing options of different colleges.

College Name: _______________________________

____

____

____

____

College Name: _______________________________

____

____

____

____

College Name: _______________________________

____

____

____

____

Chapter Conclusion

Your living situation can significantly impact your college experience, affecting everything from academic performance to personal well-being. By carefully considering the housing options, policies, and environments at each college, you can make an informed decision that aligns with your preferences and needs. Remember to balance practical considerations like cost and location with personal preferences for community and independence.

STEP 01

Research Housing Options: Visit the housing sections of college websites for detailed information.

STEP 02

Contact Housing Offices: Reach out with specific questions or to discuss accommodations.

STEP 03

Finalize Your Priorities: Update your rankings as you gather more information.

STEP 04

Prepare for Your Roommate Search: Plan how you will find your roommate(s) and how you will set yourself up for a successful roommate experience.

EMBRACE THE JOURNEY

Finding the right place to live is an exciting part of preparing for college. Stay proactive, keep an open mind, and choose a housing option that will support your success and happiness during this transformative time.

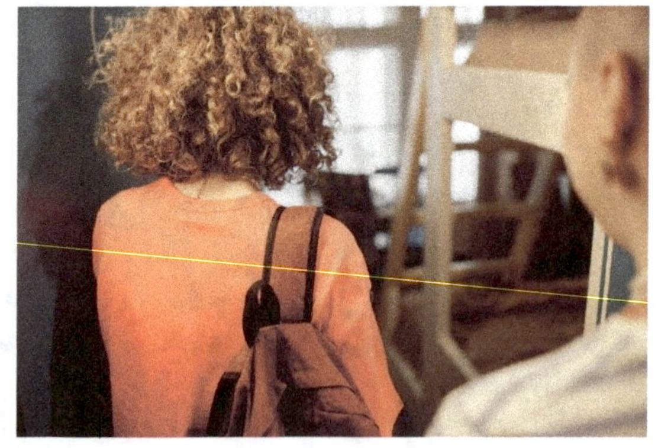

Chapter 5: College Admission Requirements

As you narrow down your list of potential colleges, it's crucial to recognize that the selection process is a two-way street. While you're evaluating which college is the right fit for you, colleges are also determining which students align with their academic standards and community values. This chapter focuses on the "reality check" of the college admissions process. We'll explore how to research and understand each college's admission requirements, acceptance rates, and other critical factors that can influence your chances of acceptance.

By proactively gathering this information, you'll be better prepared to meet application expectations and make strategic decisions about where to apply.

RESEARCHING ADMISSIONS REQUIREMENTS

Understanding the specific admission requirements of each college is essential. These requirements often include high school coursework, grade point averages (GPAs), standardized test scores, essays, recommendations, and extracurricular activities.

HIGH SCHOOL COURSEWORK REQUIREMENTS

Colleges typically have minimum coursework requirements that applicants must meet.

> **Common Coursework Requirements**
> - **English**: 4 years
> - **Mathematics**: 3-4 years (often including Algebra II and higher)
> - **Science**: 3-4 years (including lab sciences)
> - **Social Studies**: 3-4 years
> - **Foreign Language**: 2-3 years
> - **Electives**: Courses in arts, technology, or other areas

Action Steps
- **Review Your Transcript**: Ensure you're on track to meet the coursework requirements.
- **Plan for Senior Year**: If possible, adjust your course schedule to fill any gaps. You might consider alternative credit options like College Board's CLEP exams to fill in missing coursework but keep in mind not all colleges accept all forms of credit.

STANDARDIZED TEST REQUIREMENTS

Many colleges require standardized tests like the SAT or ACT, or may use these policies:
- **Test-Optional Policies**: Some schools have adopted test-optional admissions; decide if submitting scores will strengthen your application.
- **Superscoring**: Some colleges consider the highest section scores across multiple tests.

ADDITIONAL POTENTIAL REQUIREMENTS AND TIPS

- **Personal Essays:** The purpose is to showcase your personality, experiences, and writing skills. Start early, be authentic, and have others review your drafts. Avoid generic or overused responses.
- **Letters of Recommendation**: Offer an external perspective on your skills, achievements, and character through someone who knows you well. Choose recommenders who can speak to your strengths, request letters well in advance, and provide them with relevant information to write a strong endorsement.
- **Extracurricular Activities**: Target quality over quantity - having a depth of involvement and leadership roles can be more impactful. Keep a record of your activities, awards, and accomplishments.

MEETING OR EXCEEDING ADMISSION REQUIREMENTS

Here are some tips to help you meet or exceed requirements:

- **Academic Improvement**: Focus on strengthening areas where you may be below the average.
- **Test Preparation**: Invest time in studying to improve standardized test scores.
- **Enhance Your Application**: Highlight unique experiences, talents, or challenges overcome.

INTERPRETING ACCEPTANCE RATES

Knowing the acceptance rate of your targeted colleges can help you be better prepared to apply.

- **Low Acceptance Rates**: Indicates high selectivity; admissions are more competitive.
- **High Acceptance Rates**: Suggest the college is less selective; higher chances of acceptance.

Divide your college list into "safety," "match," and "reach schools based on aceptance rates and your qualifications. Balance your college list by including a diverse mix with safety, match, and reach schools to optimize options.

- **Safety Schools**: Your credentials exceed the college's average requirements.
- **Match Schools**: Your credentials closely align with the college's averages.
- **Reach Schools**: The college is highly selective, and your credentials may be below their averages.

Application Timelines
You have several options for when to submit your college applications—such as early decision, early action, regular decision, and rolling admissions. Each option comes with its own pros and cons, so it's important to understand them and choose the one that best fits your needs.

Early Action: This process allows students to submit their application early and receive early, non-binding notification of their admission decision.
Early Decision: Early decision applications are a binding commitment to enroll in the college if accepted.
Regular Decision: This is the regular decision deadline. Students will generally be notified of admission decisions in the spring.
Rolling Admissions: These institutions accept and evaluate applications on an ongoing basis until all available spots are filled.

REFLECTION EXERCISE

Are there any required courses you're missing? How can you address this? Talk to your high school counselor or a college admissions office if you need help!

____

____

How does your GPA compare to general college requirements? What strategies can you employ to improve or highlight your academic strengths?

____

____

What standardized tests do you plan to take? When are they available near you?

____

____

Tracking Admissions Information

Organizing admission requirements for each college will help you stay on top of deadlines and expectations.

ADMISSIONS REQUIREMENTS TRACKING TABLE

Use the table below to record key admissions information for each college. A larger copy of this table is available on page 107.

College Name	Courses Required	Min. GPA	Average GPA	Test Required (SAT/ACT)	Average Test Scores	Acceptance Rate	Additional Requirements

Instructions:

1. **Coursework Requirements:** Note any specific courses or years required.
2. **Minimum GPA:** The lowest GPA considered for admission.
3. **Average GPA:** The average GPA of admitted students.
4. **Test Required:** Indicate if SAT, ACT, or other tests are required or optional.
5. **Average Test Scores:** Include average scores for admitted students.
6. **Acceptance Rate:** The percentage of applicants admitted.
7. **Additional Requirements:** Essays, interviews, portfolios, etc.

Optional: Use highlighters to color code safety, match, and reach schools.

An example table is shown on the next page.

College Name	Courses Required	Min. GPA	Average GPA	Test Required (SAT/ACT)	Average Test Scores	Acceptance Rate	Additional Requirements
University A	4 Eng, 3 Math, 3 Sci, 2 FL	3.0	3.5	SAT or ACT	SAT: 1200; ACT: 25	50%	Essay, 2 recomm.
College B	4 Eng, 4 Math, 4 Sci, 3 FL	3.5	3.8	Test-Optional	N/A	20%	Essay, interview
State U C	4 Eng, 3 Math, 2 Sci, 2 SS	2.5	3.0	SAT or ACT	SAT: 1000; ACT: 20	75%	None

NOTES AND THOUGHTS

Use the space below to jot down any additional notes or reflections about the admissions requirements and your preparedness for each college.

Colleges Name ___________________

Strengths   Areas to Improve   Action Plan

___________   ___________   ________________________

___________   ___________   ________________________

Colleges Name ___________________

Strengths   Areas to Improve   Action Plan

___________   ___________   ________________________

___________   ___________   ________________________

Colleges Name ___________________

Strengths   Areas to Improve   Action Plan

___________   ___________   ________________________

___________   ___________   ________________________

Chapter Conclusion

Acknowledging the realities of college admissions is a vital step in your journey. By understanding and meeting the requirements of each institution, you enhance your chances of acceptance and reduce potential surprises. Remember that colleges are not only evaluating your academic achievements but also your potential to contribute to their community. Stay proactive, organized, and honest with yourself about where you stand and how you can present the best possible application.

STEP 01

Gather Information: Visit college websites or contact admissions offices to fill in your tracking table.

STEP 02

Assess Your Position: Compare your credentials to the colleges' averages to categorize them as safety, match, or reach schools.

STEP 03

Develop an Action Plan: Identify ways to strengthen your application where needed.

STEP 04

Stay Organized: Keep track of all deadlines and requirements in a calendar or planner.

STEP 05

Seek Guidance: Consult with your school counselor, teachers, or mentors for support.

EMBRACE THE JOURNEY

The admissions process can be challenging, but it's also an opportunity to reflect on your accomplishments and aspirations. Stay focused, be yourself, and trust that the right college fit is out there for you.

Chapter 6: Exploring College Campuses Through Visits

Now that you have thought through what you are looking for in a college, it's time to schedule visits. Visiting college campuses is a pivotal step in your college selection process. It allows you to experience firsthand the environment, culture, and resources that each institution offers. Even if you're unable to visit every college on your list, exploring nearby schools—even those not at the top of your list—can provide valuable insights into what you might prefer in a college setting. Virtual tours can also be an excellent alternative for distant schools. This chapter will guide you through making the most of campus visits, including sample questions to ask and key areas to explore.

THE VALUE OF CAMPUS VISITS

EXPERIENCING THE CAMPUS ATMOSPHERE

- **Firsthand Observation**: Get a true sense of the campus size, layout, and facilities.
- **Campus Vibe**: Feel the energy of the student body and see if it aligns with your preferences.
- **Environmental Fit**: Determine if you prefer a bustling urban campus or a serene rural setting.

COMPARING AND CONTRASTING COLLEGES

- **Identifying Common Features**: Understand what is standard across colleges (e.g., dining halls, libraries).
- **Spotting Unique Offerings**: Discover special programs, facilities, or traditions that set a college apart.

MAKING INFORMED DECISIONS

- **Clarify Preferences**: Visiting campuses can solidify what you want or don't want in a college.
- **Confidence in Choice**: Helps ensure you're making a well-informed decision about where to apply and attend.

Preparing for Your Visit

BEFORE THE VISIT

- **Schedule in Advance**: Book official campus tours, information sessions, and meetings.
- **Research**: Familiarize yourself with the college's programs and offerings.
- **Prepare Questions**: Write down questions to ask during your visit.

ITEMS TO BRING

- **Notebook and Pen**: For taking notes. Take this notebook and use the checklist at the end of this chapter!
- **Camera or Smartphone**: To capture images of the campus.
- **Comfortable Shoes:** Expect to walk a lot.

DURING THE VISIT

- **Be Observant**: Pay attention to details and how the campus makes you feel.
- **Engage**: Ask questions and interact with students and staff.
- **Take Notes**: Record your impressions and important information.

AREAS TO EXPLORE

Academic Facilities

- **Classrooms and Lecture Halls:** Observe the learning environments.
- **Libraries:** Check out study spaces and resources.
- **Laboratories:** If interested in STEM, visit science and engineering labs.
- **Studios and Practice Rooms:** For arts, music, or theater majors.

Specialized Facilities

- **Music Buildings:** For choir, instrumental practice, or lessons.
- **Theaters:** If interested in drama or performing arts.
- **Technology Centers:** Computer labs, innovation hubs.
- **Career Centers:** Resources for internships and job placement.

Student Life Spaces

- **Dormitories:** Tour different types of housing.
- **Dining Halls:** Sample the food and assess meal options.
- **Recreational Facilities:** Gyms, sports complexes, swimming pools.
- **Student Centers:** Hubs for student activities and organizations.

Surrounding Areas

- **Local Community:** Explore nearby shops, restaurants, and entertainment.
- **Transportation Options:** Check availability of public transit or campus shuttles.
- **Safety:** Observe campus security measures and general neighborhood safety.

Be sure to spend time during your visit talking to current students as well as key faculty and staff, including academic department representatives, admission counselors, and financial aid officers. Use the sample questions on this page or write down your own to be prepared before the visit.

QUESTIONS FOR TOUR GUIDES

Campus Life
- What do students do on weekends?
- How would you describe the campus culture?
- What traditions or events are unique to this college?

Academics
- What is the average class size?
- How accessible are professors outside of class?
- Are there opportunities for undergraduate research or internships?

Support Services
- What resources are available for academic support?
- How does the college support student wellness and mental health?
- What career services are offered to students?

QUESTIONS FOR FINANCIAL AID

Costs and Aid
- What is the total cost of attendance, including potential fees?
- What types of scholarships and grants are available?
- How does the college support students in finding external scholarships?

Work Opportunities
- Are there work-study programs or campus jobs?
- How flexible are work schedules with academic commitments?

Financial Planning
- Can you provide an estimate of my financial aid package?
- How does the college handle changes in a family's financial situation?

QUESTIONS FOR ADMISSIONS OFFICE

Application Process
- What are the most important factors in your admissions decisions?
- Do you have any tips for strengthening my application?
- How does the college view standardized test scores, especially if test-optional?

Deadlines and Policies
- What are the deadlines for applications, financial aid, and scholarships?
- Are there early action or early decision options?

Student Fit
- What qualities are you looking for in prospective students?
- How would you describe the ideal candidate for this college?

Personal Experience

- What do you like most and least about the college?
- How did you adjust to college life?
- What do you wish you had known before attending?

Academics

- How challenging are the courses?
- Are professors supportive and engaging?
- How manageable is the workload?

Social Life

- What clubs or organizations are popular?
- How inclusive is the campus community?
- What do students do for fun?

ADDITIONAL QUESTIONS

____

____

____

____

____

____

____

____

____

____

MAKING THE MOST OF YOUR VISIT

PERSONALIZE YOUR TOUR

- **Visit Specific Departments:** Arrange to see areas relevant to your interests.
- **Attend a Class:** Sit in on a lecture to experience the academic environment.
- **Eat on Campus:** Try the dining options available to students.

OBSERVE AND REFLECT

- **Student Interactions**: Watch how students engage with each other and staff.
- **Campus Maintenance:** Note the cleanliness and upkeep of facilities.
- **Bulletin Boards and Flyers**: See what events and activities are happening.

TIPS FOR VIRTUAL VISITS

- **Maximize Online Resources**:
  - Interactive Maps: Explore the campus layout virtually.
  - Video Tours: Watch guided tours highlighting key areas.
  - Webinars: Attend live sessions with admissions staff or faculty.
  - Student Blogs and Vlogs: Get personal perspectives from current students.
- **Ask Questions**: Use the same questions you would ask in person.
- **Technical Aspects**: Ensure you have a reliable internet connection and necessary software.
- **Engagement**: Participate actively, ask questions, and take notes.

AFTER THE VISIT

- **Review Your Notes**: While the experience is fresh, summarize your impressions.
- **Pros and Cons List**: Identify what you liked and didn't like.
- **Follow Up**: Send thank-you emails to anyone who was particularly helpful.

Which Colleges Should You Visit?

Any college you're interested in is worth a visit if possible. If not, virtual visits can also be very informative. Visiting multiple local colleges can give you great perspective on what is common and what is unique at different schools.

Local Visits

- Start Nearby: Visit colleges in your area to practice evaluating campuses.
- Broad Exposure: Even if the schools aren't your top choices, they can provide context.

Farther Away Colleges

- Schedule Visits: If possible, plan trips to colleges farther from home.
- Virtual Tours: Utilize online resources if in-person visits aren't feasible.

CAMPUS VISIT CHECKLIST

Make a copy of this page for each college visit. Use in conjunction with the campus visit observations on the next page.

College Name _______________________   **Date of Visit** _______________

AREAS TO EXPLORE: MUST SEE LIST

Here are some of the top areas to explore during your visit. Add your own based on reflections in Chapter 3.

- ☐ Classrooms
- ☐ Lecture Halls
- ☐ Library
- ☐ Dormitories
- ☐ Rec Centers
- ☐ Student Centers
- ☐ Dining Halls
- ☐ Student Resources
- ☐ _______________
- ☐ _______________
- ☐ _______________
- ☐ _______________

RANK CAMPUS FEATURES

Rank these campus features

- ☆☆☆☆☆ Cleanliness
- ☆☆☆☆☆ Friendliness
- ☆☆☆☆☆ Tech resources
- ☆☆☆☆☆ Classrooms
- ☆☆☆☆☆ Study areas
- ☆☆☆☆☆ Campus housing
- ☆☆☆☆☆ Campus resources

ADDITIONAL PLACES TO EXPLORE

✓ SURROUNDING AREA

Take a look at the community, off campus housing options, and recreational opportunities.

✓ MAJOR SPECIFIC AREAS

Look at laboratories for STEM majors, studios for music majors, etc.

✓ SAFETY

Take note of safety culture on campus. Look for security measures on campus facilities and dormitories.

✓ TRANSPORTATION

Look for available parking, bus routes, and other transportation options.

WHO TO TALK TO

Be sure to visit with representatives for offices below. Keep track of contact information as these will be helpful contacts if you choose to go to this college.

- ☐ Admissions
- ☐ Financial Aid
- ☐ Major-specific department heads
- ☐ Religious or Spiritual leaders
- ☐ _______________________
- ☐ _______________________

CAMPUS VISIT OBSERVATIONS

Make a copy of this page for each college visit. Use in conjunction with the campus visit checklist on the previous page.

College Name _______________________________   **Date of Visit** _______________________

Impressions of Campus: ____

____

____

____

Facilities Visited: ____

____

____

____

People Met (Record names, contact info, and notes): ________________

____

____

____

____

Key Takeaways: ____

____

____

Additional Notes: ____

____

____

____

____

Chapter Conclusion

Campus visits, whether in person or virtual, are invaluable for gaining deeper insight into the colleges you're considering. They allow you to go beyond brochures and websites to experience the environment, culture, and community firsthand. By preparing thoughtful questions, exploring areas of personal interest, and engaging with the campus community, you'll be better equipped to determine which college is the best fit for you.

STEP 01

Plan Your Visits: Schedule campus tours, information sessions, and meetings.

STEP 02

Prepare Questions: Customize the sample questions provided to suit your interests.

STEP 03

Engage During Visits: Be active, observant, and open-minded.

STEP 04

Document Your Experiences: Use the provided checklist and notes sections.

STEP 05

Reflect and Compare: Use your observations to distinguish between your college options.

EMBRACE THE JOURNEY

Each campus visit brings you one step closer to finding your college home. Enjoy the process of exploration and discovery, and trust your instincts about where you'll thrive.

Section I Conclusion

Congratulations on taking these significant steps toward choosing the college that's right for you. Throughout this section, you've explored various crucial aspects—from financial priorities and academic programs to social life, housing, admissions requirements, and campus visits. Now it's time to synthesize this information to aid in your decision-making process.

ASSIGNING POINTS AND RANKING COLLEGES

1. **Define a Scoring Scale**: Use a consistent scale for all categories (e.g., 1 to 5, where 5 is the highest satisfaction).
2. **Evaluate Each Category**: For each college, rate the financial fit, available academic programs and majors, social scene, housing options, admissions alignment, and your impression of the campus.
3. **Calculate Total Scores**: Sum the points for each college to get a total score.

A larger copy of this table is available on page 108.

College Name	Financial Fit	Academics	Social Scene	Housing	Admissions Fit	Campus Feel	Total Score

An example table is shown below. Tips are included on the next page for more information.

College Name	Financial Fit	Academics	Social Scene	Housing	Admissions Fit	Campus Feel	Total Score
University A	2 – high tuition	5 – has the program I want	3 – missing clubs I want	4 – nice dorms	3 – stretch school	5 – beautiful and friendly	22
State College B	4 – low tuition	5 – has the program I want	5 – great fellowship program	2 – dorms could be better	5 – match school	3 – clean but not as friendly	23

REFLECTING ON THE RANKINGS

- **Identify Top Contenders**: Based on total scores, see which colleges rank highest.
- **Analyze the Results**: Look for patterns or categories where certain colleges excel or fall short.
- **Balance Objectivity and Subjectivity**: Remember that numbers don't capture everything.

ADJUSTING SCORES

If you feel like the rankings don't match your feelings, you may need to adjust the scales. If you have one or two categories that are more important than the others, try giving these categories a multiplier. For example, if the campus feel is the most important to you, use a 2x multiplier. In the example on the previous page, that would change University A's campus feel to a 10 and the final score would be 27; meanwhile, State College B would have a campus feel score of 6 and a final score of 26, changing the highest scoring college to University A.

TRUSTING YOUR GUT FEELINGS

While quantitative scores provide a structured comparison, your intuition and feelings are equally important.

- **Listen to Your Instincts**: If a college feels like the right place for you, that's significant.
- **Consider Unquantifiable Factors**: Campus atmosphere, personal interactions, and overall comfort can't always be measured.
- **Acknowledge Mixed Feelings**: It's okay if a highly ranked college doesn't feel like the perfect fit.
- **Admission Decisions**: Keep in mind, you also have to be accepted by the college. It's good to keep an open mind until you know what your final options are.

SPACE FOR PERSONAL REFLECTIONS

____

____

____

____

____

____

____

Final Thoughts

Choosing a college is a deeply personal decision that will shape your future in many ways. By thoroughly evaluating each aspect and trusting your instincts, you're well on your way to finding the college that will become your home for the next few years.

MAKING YOUR DECISION

Remember, the goal of this process is to empower you to make an informed and confident choice.

- **Balance Data and Emotion**: Use both your rankings and your personal reflections.
- **Seek Advice**: Discuss your thoughts with mentors, family, or trusted friends.
- **Be Open-Minded**: Allow yourself the flexibility to reconsider as you gain new insights.
- **Re-evaluate if necessary:** While students would like to find the perfect fit on the first try, if you find a college is not working out, you CAN change your mind!
  - If this happens to you, be sure to work with mentors, parents, and/or academic advisors to smooth the transition to a new school.

EMBRACE THE JOURNEY

Trust that you have the tools and self-awareness to make the choice that's right for you. Whatever decision you make, it's the beginning of an exciting new chapter in your life.

Section II

Congratulations on taking the significant step of planning your college journey! Now that you've explored how to choose the right college, it's time to focus on setting meaningful goals for your time there. This section is dedicated to helping you establish, pursue, and periodically reassess your personal and academic objectives during college.

It's time to focus
on setting
meaningful
goals

Quick Note About Goal Setting

As you move into the goal setting section of this workbook, keep the **SMART** goal setting method in mind. Created by George Doran in the 1980's, **SMART** goals are **S**pecific, **M**easureable, **A**ttainable, **R**elevant, and **T**ime-bound. If you are unfamiliar with this goal setting framework, take a few moments now to research and learn more. While not all of the aspects of the **SMART** goals will apply to each of the goal you're setting here, it is good to keep the framework in mind to make sure your goals are set to have meaningful impact.

THE DYNAMIC NATURE OF GOALS

As you enter this new phase of life, it's important to recognize that your goals may change —and that's perfectly normal. College is a time of immense growth, exploration, and self-discovery. You will encounter new ideas, experiences, and challenges that can reshape your perspectives and aspirations.

- **Remember**: We can't possibly predict everything we will learn, feel, or experience during our young adult years, whether or not we attend college. *Embracing change is part of the journey.*

REGULAR REFLECTION AND REASSESSMENT

To ensure your goals remain aligned with your evolving self, we encourage you to revisit them regularly. **Right now, before you forget, set a reminder in your calendar to review your goals every six months.** This practice will help you:

- **Track Progress**: See how far you've come and celebrate your achievements.
- **Adapt to Change**: Modify goals that no longer fit your vision or set new ones that inspire you.
- **Stay Focused**: Keep your priorities clear amid the many distractions college life can bring.

EMBRACE GROWTH AND CHANGE

As you progress through college, be open to the growth that comes with new experiences. Your goals should be living documents that evolve as you do. This approach not only keeps your objectives relevant but also makes your journey more fulfilling.

Let's Begin!

Turn the page to start setting goals that will shape your college experience and lay the foundation for your future. Remember, this is your journey—embrace it with enthusiasm, curiosity, and an open mind.

Chapter 7: Reflecting on Your Personal Values and Habits

As you embark on your college journey, it's essential to take a moment to reflect on who you are and what matters most to you. Understanding your core values, strengths, and habits will not only help you stay grounded amidst the changes college brings but also guide you in making decisions that align with your authentic self.

This chapter invites you to delve deep into self-reflection, celebrating the traits you're proud of and identifying the habits you wish to continue nurturing. Whether it's maintaining a consistent workout routine, volunteering for causes close to your heart, or dedicating time to creative pursuits, acknowledging these aspects will set a solid foundation for your personal growth during college.

THE IMPORTANCE OF SELF-REFLECTION

Self-reflection is a powerful tool for personal development. It allows you to:

- **Gain Self-Awareness**: Understand your motivations, desires, and the factors that influence your behavior.
- **Align Actions with Values**: Ensure that your daily activities reflect what you genuinely care about.
- **Identify Growth Opportunities**: Recognize areas where you can improve or develop new skills.
- **Boost Confidence**: Acknowledge your achievements and the qualities that make you unique.

REFLECTION EXERCISES

Take some time to consider the qualities and characteristics that define you. Answer the following prompts:

TRAITS I'M PROUD OF

____

____

____

VALUES THAT GUIDE ME

____

____

____

STRENGTHS OTHERS ADMIRE IN ME

____

____

____

If you're having a hard time coming up with traits, values, or strengths, try reaching out to a parent, mentor, or friend for help. Sometimes others can see us more clearly than we see ourselves.

PERSONAL VALUES ASSESSMENT

Consider what matters most to you in life. Below is a list of common values. Check the ones that resonate with you, and add any others that are important to you:

- ☐ Integrity
- ☐ Compassion
- ☐ Creativity
- ☐ Responsibility
- ☐ Adventure
- ☐ Learning
- ☐ Community
- ☐ Health
- ☐ _______________
- ☐ _______________

- ☐ Family
- ☐ Independence
- ☐ Faith
- ☐ Justice
- ☐ Friendship
- ☐ Sustainability
- ☐ Excellence
- ☐ _______________
- ☐ _______________
- ☐ _______________

RECOGNIZING HABITS TO CONTINUE

Your habits shape your daily life and contribute to your overall well-being. Identifying positive habits you wish to maintain can help you stay balanced during college.

HEALTHY HABITS I WANT TO CONTINUE

_________________________ _________________________

_________________________ _________________________

ACTIVITIES THAT BRING ME JOY

_________________________ _________________________

_________________________ _________________________

WAYS I CURRENTLY CONTRIBUTE TO MY COMMUNITY

_________________________ _________________________

_________________________ _________________________

ACTION STEPS TO ACHIEVE YOUR GOALS

On the next page, you will start laying out a few personal goals. Here are tips to help you to stick with your goals.

1. **Create a Schedule**
   - **Plan Ahead:** Use a planner or digital calendar to allocate time for your habits and activities.
   - **Consistency is Key:** Establish regular times each week dedicated to your goals.
2. **Find Resources and Support**
   - **Campus Facilities:** Identify gyms, art studios, or volunteering centers on campus.
   - **Join Clubs or Groups:** Connect with student organizations that align with your interests.
   - **Accountability Partners:** Find friends or peers who share your goals.
3. **Set Reminders**
   - **Digital Alerts:** Set notifications on your phone or computer.
   - **Visual Cues:** Place notes or symbols in your living space to remind you of your commitments.
4. **Monitor Progress**
   - **Journaling:** Keep a journal to reflect on your experiences and track your progress.
   - **Self-Check-ins:** Regularly assess how well you're adhering to your goals.

SETTING PERSONAL GOALS

Based on your reflections, set specific goals to maintain and enhance your positive traits and habits during college.

GOAL-SETTING WORKSHEET

Goal: (e.g., Maintain a consistent workout schedule)

____

Why This is Important to Me:

____

Action Steps:

____

____

____

Potential Challenges and Solutions:

____

____

Goal: (e.g., Continue volunteering for environmental causes)

____

Why This is Important to Me:

____

Action Steps:

____

____

____

Potential Challenges and Solutions:

____

____

SIX-MONTH REFLECTION AND UPDATE

It's time to revisit your goals and assess your progress. Use the following prompts every six months to reflect. If you need to adjust or add new goals, use the extra sheets included at the end of the workbook.

REFLECTION PROMPTS

Which goals have I achieved or maintained?

____

____

What challenges did I encounter? How did I overcome them?

____

____

New habits or traits I've developed:

____

____

12-MONTH REFLECTION

Progress summary:

____

____

New insights:

____

____

Goals to add or adjust:

____

____

____

____

Chapter Conclusion

Reflecting on your personal values, traits, and habits is a continuous journey that evolves as you grow. By taking time to understand and honor what is important to you, you set the stage for a fulfilling college experience that aligns with your authentic self. Remember to revisit this chapter every six months, using the reflection prompts to stay connected with your evolving identity. Embrace the changes that come with new experiences, and allow your goals to adapt accordingly.

STEP 01

Complete the Reflection Exercises: Identify your core traits, values, and habits.

STEP 02

Set Specific Goals: Use the goal-setting worksheet to outline actionable steps.

STEP 03

Implement Action Steps: Create schedules, find resources, and monitor progress.

STEP 04

Set Calendar Reminders: Schedule six-month intervals for goal review.

STEP 05

Reflect and Adjust: Use the provided prompts to assess and modify your goals.

EMBRACE THE JOURNEY

Your college years are a time of incredible growth and self-discovery. Stay true to yourself, remain open to new experiences, and let your values guide you toward the person you aspire to be.

Chapter 8: Aligning Your Values with Your College Experience

Understanding and embracing your personal values is a cornerstone of personal development and fulfillment. Your values guide your decisions, influence your behavior, and shape your interactions with others. In college, you'll encounter new situations, challenges, and opportunities that will test and refine these values.

This chapter builds upon your reflections by helping you identify your core values and set specific goals that align with them. By consciously integrating your values into your college life, you'll navigate this transformative period with integrity and purpose.

DISCOVERING YOUR CORE VALUES

The Importance of Knowing Your Values
- **Guidance in Decision-Making**: Values serve as a compass, helping you make choices that align with who you are.
- **Consistency in Behavior**: They ensure that your actions are consistent across different situations.
- **Fulfillment and Satisfaction**: Living according to your values leads to a more satisfying and meaningful life.

CORE VALUE QUIZ

The next pages contain a quiz to help identify your core values. For each question, choose the option (A, B, C, or D) that best represents what you would do. After completing the quiz, use the scoring sheet to tally your selections and discover your top personal values.

1.The Lost Wallet
You find a wallet on the street filled with cash and the owner's ID. What do you do?
A) Return it to the owner intact.
B) Take the cash and leave the wallet where you found it.
C) Donate the money to someone in need and return the wallet.
D) Keep the money and the wallet; finders keepers!

2. Career Crossroads

You have a stable job but are offered a position in a startup that excites you but lacks security. What do you choose?

A) Stick with your stable job for security.

B) Take the startup job for new challenges.

C) Weigh the options carefully before deciding.

D) Decline both and consider starting your own venture.

3. Friend in Need

A close friend needs help moving on the same day you planned a relaxing day for yourself. What do you do?

A) Help your friend; friendship comes first.

B) Politely decline; you need time for yourself.

C) Help for a few hours, then enjoy your day.

D) Hire movers for your friend so you can keep your plans.

4. The Group Project

In a team project, you notice others aren't contributing equally. What do you do?

A) Take charge to ensure the project's success.

B) Do your part and let others face the consequences.

C) Address the issue with the team openly.

D) Inform the supervisor about the lack of contribution.

5. The Ethical Dilemma

Your company is dumping waste illegally, harming the environment. What do you do?

A) Report it to authorities, even if it risks your job.

B) Ignore it to protect your position.

C) Discuss your concerns with your manager.

D) Seek a new job and then report it anonymously.

6. Family Expectations

Your family wants you to pursue a traditional career, but you have a passion for the arts. What do you do?

A) Follow your passion despite their wishes.

B) Choose the traditional path to honor your family.

C) Try to balance both paths.

D) Find a way to convince your family to support your passion.

7. The Misunderstanding

You hear a rumor that a colleague is speaking ill of you. What do you do?

A) Confront them directly to clear the air.

B) Ignore it; you don't engage in drama.

C) Discuss it with a mutual friend for advice.

D) Reflect on your actions to see if there's any truth to it.

8. The Donation Decision

You have some extra money this month. Do you:

A) Save it for future security.

B) Spend it on an experience or item you've wanted.

C) Donate it to a charity you support.

D) Invest it in a personal development course.

9. Cultural Differences

A new neighbor from a different culture moves in next door. Do you:

A) Welcome them and learn about their culture.

B) Keep to yourself; everyone needs personal space.

C) Organize a neighborhood gathering to introduce them.

D) Offer assistance if they need anything.

10. The Unfair Advantage

You have access to information that could help you win a competition. What do you do?

A) Use it; winning is important.

B) Refrain; it's not fair to others.

C) Share the information with all participants.

D) Inform the organizers about the leak.

11. The Missed Call

You promised to call a friend but forgot. They seem upset. How do you handle it?

A) Apologize sincerely and reschedule.

B) Explain that you've been very busy.

C) Send a text instead; it's quicker.

D) Surprise them with a visit to make up for it.

12. The Team Victory

Your team wins a competition thanks to your significant contribution, but the leader takes all the credit. What do you do?

A) Let it go; the team's success is what matters.

B) Address it privately with the leader.

C) Seek recognition by mentioning your contribution publicly.

D) Plan to work independently next time.

Use the key below to identify the values represented by each of your choices from the quiz. Then, use the tally sheet to record how many times you chose each value.

Question 1:
- A) Integrity
- B) Self-Interest
- C) Compassion
- D) Independence

Question 2:
- A) Security
- B) Adventure
- C) Responsibility
- D) Creativity

Question 3:
- A) Loyalty
- B) Personal Growth
- C) Harmony
- D) Compassion

Question 4:
- A) Leadership
- B) Independence
- C) Harmony
- D) Justice

Question 5:
- A) Integrity
- B) Security
- C) Responsibility
- D) Courage

Question 6:
- A) Ambition
- B) Loyalty
- C) Harmony
- D) Independence

Question 7:
- A) Courage
- B) Independence
- C) Harmony
- D) Personal Growth

Question 8:
- A) Security
- B) Adventure
- C) Compassion
- D) Personal Growth

Question 9:
- A) Harmony
- B) Independence
- C) Leadership
- D) Compassion

Question 10:
- A) Ambition
- B) Integrity
- C) Justice
- D) Responsibility

Question 11:
- A) Integrity
- B) Ambition
- C) Independence
- D) Compassion

Question 12:
- A) Harmony
- B) Justice
- C) Ambition
- D) Independence

Tally Sheet:

______ Integrity	______ Loyalty	______ Leadership
______ Ambition	______ Independence	______ Courage
______ Compassion	______ Creativity	______ Personal Growth
______ Adventure	______ Responsibility	______ Justice
______ Security	______ Harmony	

Identify Your Top Values:

The values with the highest counts on the tally sheet are your core personal values. If multiple values have the same high count, they are equally significant to you.

Here's a brief explanation of each value:

Integrity: Adherence to moral and ethical principles; honesty.

Ambition: Strong desire to achieve, typically requiring determination and hard work.

Compassion: Sympathetic consciousness of others' distress with a desire to alleviate it.

Adventure: Willingness to take risks and try new methods, ideas, or experiences.

Security: Desire for safety, stability, and freedom from fear or anxiety.

Justice: Just behavior or treatment; fairness.

Loyalty: A strong feeling of support or allegiance.

Independence: Freedom from outside control or support; self-sufficiency.

Creativity: Use of imagination or original ideas to create something; inventiveness.

Responsibility: Being accountable for something within one's power or control.

Harmony: Agreement or concord; living in peace with others.

Personal Growth: Ongoing process of understanding and developing oneself to achieve one's fullest potential.

Leadership: The ability to guide and inspire others toward achieving a common goal.

Courage: The strength to face fear, uncertainty, or adversity with confidence and determination.

EXAMPLES OF VALUES IN ACTION

Now that you've identified some core values, you might be wondering what committing to those values might look like. Here are some examples of what purposeful commitment to a few of these values might look like.

Integrity in Action

- **Academic Integrity**: Commit to original work, avoid plagiarism, and uphold honesty in exams and assignments. Familiarize yourself with the college's academic integrity guidelines.
- **Time Management**: Schedule study times and keep track of due dates to reduce stress and the temptation to cut corners. Use a planner or digital calendar to track assignments and exams.
- **Open Communication**: Be truthful in your interactions with peers, professors, and staff.
- **Seek Help When Needed**: Utilize tutoring centers or office hours to overcome academic challenges.

Personal Growth in Action
- **Continuous Learning:** Take courses outside your major that interest you. Enroll in classes that challenge or excite you.
- **Workshops and Seminars:** Attend events that develop new skills or perspectives. Participate in lectures, cultural events, or discussions.
- **Self-Reflection:** Regularly assess your experiences and growth. Keep a journal to document your thoughts, experiences, and lessons learned.

Compassion in Action
- **Empathy Development**: Practice active listening to understand others' feelings and perspectives.
- **Community Service**: Engage in volunteer work to support those in need. Join local charities or campus organizations focused on helping others.
- **Supportive Relationships**: Cultivate kindness and offer help to peers and community members. Participate in seminars on emotional intelligence and compassionate communication.
- **Practice Kindness Daily**: Perform small acts that make a positive impact on someone's day.

SETTING AND IMPLEMENTING VALUES-BASED GOALS

Now it's time to identify some values-based goals you would like to achieve while at college. Before you dive into writing your goals, here are some tips for how to implement those goals and to help you determine which goals are right for you.

STRATEGIES FOR SUCCESS

1. Integrate Values into Daily Life
- **Mindful Decision-Making**: Pause to consider how choices align with your values.
- **Value Reminders**: Keep visual cues in your living space or digital devices.

2. Engage with Like-Minded Communities
- **Join Clubs and Organizations**: Find groups that share your values.
- **Attend Events**: Participate in workshops, lectures, or gatherings focused on your interests.

3. Seek Support and Accountability
- **Mentors**: Connect with faculty or staff who can guide you.
- **Peer Groups**: Form study groups or support networks with classmates.
- **Counseling Services**: Utilize campus resources for personal development.

4. Reflect Regularly
- **Journaling**: Write about your experiences and how they relate to your values.
- **Self-Assessment**: Periodically evaluate your adherence to your values.

SETTING GOALS ALIGNED WITH YOUR VALUES

For each of your top values, set a specific, actionable goal that you can work toward during your college years.

GOAL-SETTING WORKSHEET

Value: ____

Goal: e.g., If the value is "Integrity" the goal might be "Maintain academic integrity by adhering to all university policies and avoiding plagiarism."

____

Why This is Important to Me:

____

Action Steps:

    ____

    ____

    ____

Potential Challenges and Solutions:

____

____

Value: ____

Goal: e.g., If the value is "Courage" the goal might be "Take a speech class this semester to help overcome my fear of public speaking."

____

Why This is Important to Me:

____

Action Steps:

    ____

    ____

    ____

Potential Challenges and Solutions:

____

____

SIX-MONTH REFLECTION AND UPDATE

It's time to revisit your goals and assess your progress. Use the following prompts every six months to reflect.

REFLECTION PROMPTS

Have I been living according to my core values? Provide examples.

____

____

Which goals have I achieved or made progress towards? What challenges have I faced?

____

____

Have any of my values shifted or evolved?

____

____

12-MONTH REFLECTION

Progress summary:

____

____

New insights:

____

____

Goals to add or adjust:

____

____

____

Chapter Conclusion

Your values are integral to who you are and who you will become during your college journey. By identifying and actively living according to your core values, you ensure that your college experience is not only successful academically but also fulfilling personally.

Remember to:

- **Set Specific Goals**: Align your actions with your values through clear objectives.
- **Take Action**: Implement strategies to integrate your values into daily life.
- **Reflect and Adjust**: Revisit your values and goals regularly, adapting as needed.

STEP 01

Complete the Values Quiz: Identify your top core values.

STEP 02

Set Goals and Implement Strategies: Use the goal-setting worksheet to outline actionable steps and apply the suggested strategies to live your values.

STEP 03

Schedule Regular Reflections: Set reminders for six-month reviews.

STEP 04

Adjust as Needed: Be open to evolving your goals over time.

EMBRACE THE JOURNEY

Living authentically according to your values will enrich your college experience and contribute to your personal growth. Stay true to yourself, and let your values guide you toward a purposeful and rewarding college life.

Chapter 9: Setting Financial Goals for Future Success

Financial well-being is a critical component of your college experience and long-term success. Building upon the financial considerations you explored in the first section, this chapter focuses on setting practical financial goals for your time in college. By proactively managing your finances, you can reduce debt, earn income, and develop habits that will serve you well beyond graduation.

Whether you're looking to earn money through part-time work, minimize expenses, or find creative ways to save, establishing clear financial objectives will help you navigate college with confidence and less stress. This chapter provides guidance on setting these goals, actionable steps to achieve them, and reflection prompts to adjust your plans as needed.

THE IMPORTANCE OF FINANCIAL GOALS IN COLLEGE

Benefits of Financial Planning

- **Reduce Stress**: Alleviate the anxiety associated with money management.
- **Avoid Excessive Debt**: Minimize student loans and credit card debt.
- **Build Financial Literacy**: Gain skills that are essential for post-college life.
- **Achieve Independence**: Take control of your financial future.

In the first section, you assessed the financial aspects of choosing a college, including costs, loans, and scholarships. Now, it's time to focus on managing your finances while in college to ensure you stay on track with your broader financial objectives.

Consider what you want to achieve financially during your college years. Your goals might include earning income, reducing or avoiding debt, and developing saving habits.

EXAMPLE GOALS AND HOW TO ACHIEVE THEM

GOAL 1: EARNING MONEY DURING COLLEGE

Earning income while in college can help cover expenses, reduce the need for loans, and provide valuable work experience.

Opportunities to Earn Money

1. Part-Time Jobs
- On-campus employment can include positions in libraries, cafeterias, administrative offices.
- Off-campus jobs can include retail, restaurants, tutoring, or service industry roles.

2. Work-Study Programs
- Federal Work-Study is a program providing part-time jobs for students with financial need.

3. Internships
- Paid internships can help you gain industry experience and earn money.

4. Freelancing and Gig Economy
- Opportunities can include writing, graphic design, programming, virtual assistance. ridesharing, food delivery, or pet sitting.

Action Steps for Earning Money

1. Explore Job Opportunities
- Find your college's campus job board, check local businesses, and search online platforms.

2. Prepare Application Materials
- Create a resume to highlight skills and experience; write a cover letter tailored to each position you apply for. Check for resources at your college to help.

3. Time Management
- Determine how many hours per week you can work without compromising academics. Use a planner to balance work, study, and personal time.

Potential Challenges and Solutions

1. **Challenge**: Balancing work and academics
   - **Solution**: Limit work hours; priortize time management.
2. **Challenge**: Lack of experience.
   - **Solution**: Emphasize transferable skills; seek entry-level position and ask for help through college resources.

Minimizing debt will ease your financial burden after graduation.

Strategies to Reduce Debt

1. Budgeting
- Track income and expenses by using apps or spreadsheets.
- Identify non-essential spending; cut back on unnecessary expenses.
- Set spending limits by allocating funds for each category (food, entertainment, etc.).

2. Minimizing Expenses
- Consider cost-effective housing options.
- Plan meals ahead of time; cook at home or use college meal plans wisely.
- Save on textbook costs by buying used books, renting, or using library copies.

3. Seeking Scholarships and Grants
- Apply to scholarships yearly; continue searching for scholarships throughout college.
- Check with your academic department for major-specific opportunities.
- Look for grants from local businesses, community organizations, or nonprofits.

4. Loan Management Strategies
- Understand your loans by knowing the terms, interest rates, and repayment plans.
- Avoid unnecessary borrowing by only taking what you need.
- If possible, make interest payments on loans while in school to reduce overall debt.

Action Steps for Reducing Debt

1. Create a Detailed Budget
- Record and track your income sources, fixed expenses, and variable expenses.

2. Scholarship Applications
- Use online, college, and local resources to identify scholarship opportunities. Revisit Chapter 1 to track scholarship applications. Don't forget to reapply every year!

3. Loan Review
- Keep track of your loans, the interest rates, and repayment options. Don't wait until after graduation to start thinking about loans repayment.

Potential Challenges and Solutions

1. **Challenge**: Sticking to a budget
   - **Solution**: Set realistic limits; allow for small indulgences to prevent burnout.
2. **Challenge**: Finding scholarships.
   - **Solution**: Schedule regular time for scholarship searches and applications. Revisit Chapter 1 for more scholarship tips and tracking.

What are my primary financial concerns for college?

____

____

What do I want to achieve financially by the time I graduate?

____

____

List three specific financial goals:

1. ____

2. ____

3. ____

Use the space below to jot down any additional thoughts, plans, or resources you want to explore.

- **Resources to Explore**:

____

____

____

- **People to Consult (Financial Aid Officers, Mentors, etc.):**

____

____

____

SIX-MONTH REFLECTION AND UPDATE

Set a reminder to review your financial goals every six months. Reflect on your progress and make adjustments as needed.

REFLECTION PROMPTS

Have I met my financial goals?

____

____

What challenges have I faced?

____

____

Have any of my goals changed?

____

____

12-MONTH REFLECTION

Progress summary:

____

____

New insights:

____

____

Goals to add or adjust:

____

____

____

____

Chapter Conclusion

Setting and pursuing financial goals during college is a significant step toward achieving long-term financial stability and independence. By earning income, managing and reducing debt, and cultivating saving habits, you'll not only alleviate financial stress but also equip yourself with valuable skills for the future. As you work towards financial stability, utilize campus resources and seek advice from trusted individuals.

ADDITIONAL TIPS FOR FINANCIAL SUCCESS

Building Financial Literacy
- **Educational Resources**: Attend workshops or seminars on financial management.
- **Books and Podcasts**: Seek out materials focused on personal finance.
- **Online Courses**: Utilize free or low-cost courses to enhance your knowledge.

Credit Management
- **Understand Credit Scores**: Learn how credit works and its impact on your future.
- **Use Credit Wisely**: If you have a credit card, keep balances low and pay on time.
- **Monitor Credit Reports**: Check your credit report annually for accuracy.

Emergency Fund
- **Purpose**: Set aside funds for unexpected expenses.
- **Goal Amount**: Aim for $500 to $1,000 initially.

STEP 01

Define Your Financial Goals: Use the reflection exercise to identify what you want to achieve.

STEP 02

Educate Yourself: Build your financial literacy through available resources.

STEP 03

Set Reminders for Reflection: Schedule six-month check-ins to review and adjust your goals.

EMBRACE THE JOURNEY

Financial management is a lifelong skill that will benefit you well beyond your college years. Stay committed to your goals, be adaptable, and remember that every small step contributes to your overall financial well-being.

Chapter 10: Setting Social Goals for a Fulfilling Experience

College is not just about academics; it's also a time to build lasting relationships, explore new interests, and develop social skills that will benefit you throughout your life. This chapter focuses on setting social goals that align with your interests and values, helping you to make the most of the social opportunities available in college.

Drawing from the social considerations you explored in the first section, we'll delve into how to find and engage in social events, organizations, clubs, and intramural sports that resonate with you. We'll also discuss the dynamics of living with roommates, setting expectations, and fostering positive relationships in shared living spaces.

By setting clear social goals and actively seeking out opportunities, you'll enhance your college experience, build a supportive community, and develop interpersonal skills that are essential for personal and professional success.

EXPLORING SOCIAL OPPORTUNITIES

Identifying Your Social Interests
Before you can set social goals, it's important to understand what types of social activities and communities you are interested in. Revisit Chapter 3 and write down the activities and hobbies you identified here.

____

____

____

New Activities and Hobbies
Are there any activities or hobbies you would like to try while in college? Add those here.

____

____

____

Most colleges offer a wide array of social opportunities. Here are some ways to discover what's available:

1. Campus Involvement Fairs

- At the beginning of each semester, colleges often host fairs where student organizations set up booths to recruit new members. Attend the involvement fair and speak with representatives from clubs that interest you.

2. Student Organization Directories

- Many colleges maintain an online directory of student organizations. Browse the directory to identify groups you'd like to join.

3. Campus Event Calendars

- Check the college's online calendar or app for upcoming events, workshops, and social gatherings. Mark events of interest on your personal calendar and plan to attend.

4. Intramural Sports

- Intramural sports leagues offer a fun, low-pressure way to stay active and meet new people. Sign up for a sport you enjoy or try a new one.

5. Fraternities and Sororities

- Greek life organizations focus on brotherhood/sisterhood, philanthropy, and social activities. Research the fraternities and sororities on campus to see if they align with your values and interests.

6. Special Interest and Cultural Clubs

- Look for clubs based on shared interests, identities, or cultural backgrounds. Join clubs that celebrate your heritage or explore new cultures.

7. Volunteer Opportunities

- Engage with the community through service projects. Participate in volunteer events organized by the college or local nonprofits.

Tips for Getting Involved

- **Start Early:** The beginning of the semester is a great time to join clubs when new members are being recruited.
- **Be Open-Minded:** Try activities outside your comfort zone to expand your horizons.
- **Balance:** Ensure you have a manageable schedule that doesn't overwhelm your academic commitments.

SETTING SOCIAL GOALS

Based on your interests, set specific social goals for your college experience.

GOAL-SETTING WORKSHEET

Goal: (e.g., Join the campus newspaper staff to pursue my interest in journalism)

____

Action Steps: ____

____

____

Potential Challenges and Solutions:

____

____

Goal: (e.g., Find a list of intramural sports available. Try two of the sports this year.)

____

Action Steps: ____

____

____

Potential Challenges and Solutions:

____

____

Goal: (e.g., Attend at least one campus event each semester to meet new people.)

____

Action Steps: ____

____

____

Potential Challenges and Solutions:

____

____

SIX-MONTH REFLECTION AND UPDATE

Regularly assessing your social goals ensures they continue to align with your interests and experiences.

REFLECTION PROMPTS

What social goals have I achieved or made progress toward?

____

____

What new social interests have emerged?

____

____

What challenges have I faced socially, and how have I addressed them?

____

____

12-MONTH REFLECTION

Progress summary:

____

____

New insights:

____

____

Goals to add or adjust:

____

____

____

____

Navigating Roommate Relationships

Living with roommates can be one of the most rewarding or challenging aspects of college life. Regardless of your experience, it offers valuable lessons in communication, collaboration, and compromise.

SETTING EXPECTATIONS WITH ROOMMATES

Understanding Your Non-Negotiables
Before moving in with roommates, it's important to identify your non-negotiable needs and preferences.

REFLECTION EXERCISE

1. What are my must-haves in a living situation?

____

____

2. What behaviors or habits are unacceptable to me?

____

____

3. What am I willing to compromise on?

____

____

Discussing Expectations
Open communication is key to a successful roommate relationship.

Topics to Discuss:
- **Cleanliness and Chores**: How will household duties be divided?
- **Quiet Hours**: Preferred times for studying and sleeping.
- **Guests and Visitors**: Policies on having friends or partners over.
- **Shared Items**: What items are communal, and what are personal?
- **Financial Responsibilities**: How will bills and expenses be split?

CREATING A ROOMMATE AGREEMENT

A roommate agreement outlines the agreed-upon rules and expectations for living together. This is highly recommended. You may need to revisit the agreement over time, but open and honest discussion, and a willingness to compromise, is essential for a successful roommate relationship. Here are things you may want to discuss and include in your roommate agreement.

Cleaning Responsibilities
- Kitchen Duties
- Bathroom Cleaning
- General Tidiness and Upkeep
- Common Areas

Quiet Time and Guests
- Weekday Quiet Hours
- Weekend Quiet Hours
- Guest Policy
- Overnight Guests

Financial Agreements
- Rent Split
- Utilities
- Shared Purchases

Shared Items and Spaces
- Food and Groceries
- Appliances
- Electronics

Conflict Resolution
- Communication Method
- Steps for Resolving Issues
  - Example resolution steps:
  - Discuss the issue in person within 24 hours
  - If unresolved, involve a neutral 3rd party (e.g., RA or mutual friend)
  - Seek mediation through housing services if necessary

Resources for Finding Housing and Roommates
- **College Housing Office**: Provides listings and roommate matching services.
- **Online Platforms**: Websites and apps dedicated to roommate matching (e.g., Roomsurf, RoomSync).
- **Social Media Groups**: College-specific social media groups or forums.
- **Bulletin Boards**: Physical boards on campus where students post housing ads.

Tips for Successful Coexistence
- **Open Communication**: Regularly check in with your roommates.
- **Respect Differences**: Acknowledge and appreciate diverse backgrounds and lifestyles.
- **Flexibility**: Be willing to adjust and compromise when needed.
- **Set Boundaries**: Know your limits and express them respectfully.

Chapter Conclusion

Setting and pursuing social goals is a vital part of creating a well-rounded and fulfilling college experience. By actively engaging in clubs, organizations, and events that interest you, you'll build a supportive community and develop essential social skills. Navigating roommate relationships with clear expectations and open communication will enhance your living environment and teach valuable life lessons.

STEP 01 — **Research Opportunities:** Utilize campus resources to find clubs, events, and organizations.

STEP 02 — **Set Social Goals:** Outline specific, actionable goals related to your social life.

STEP 03 — **Navigate Roommate Relationships:** Establish expectations, create a roommate agreement, and communicate effectively.

STEP 04 — **Utilize Resources:** Access platforms and services for finding housing, roommates, and events.

STEP 05 — **Set Reminders for Reflection:** Schedule six-month check-ins to review and adjust your social goals.

EMBRACE THE JOURNEY

College offers a unique opportunity to explore new social horizons, build meaningful relationships, and develop interpersonal skills that will last a lifetime. Stay open to new experiences, be proactive in seeking out opportunities, and enjoy the vibrant social landscape of your college years.

Chapter 11: Nurturing Your Spiritual Well-being

College is a time of significant growth and change, presenting both opportunities and challenges to your personal beliefs and practices. For many, spiritual well-being is a cornerstone of identity, providing guidance, comfort, and a sense of community. As you transition into this new chapter of life, it's helpful to develop a plan to maintain and nurture your spiritual practices.

This chapter focuses on helping you stay connected to your faith while embracing the college experience. We'll explore strategies for staying in touch with your home faith community, finding new spiritual groups on campus, and setting goals to continue your practice. By proactively planning, you'll equip yourself to make choices that align with your beliefs and values, ensuring that your spiritual well-being remains a source of strength during your college years.

Note: This chapter is meant to provide guidance for individuals looking to maintain their personal beliefs and practices during college. The strategies mentioned can be adapted to fit various beliefs and should be tailored to your specific needs and circumstances.

THE IMPORTANCE OF MAINTAINING SPIRITUAL PRACTICES

Recognizing the Temporary Nature of College
- College is a temporary phase, but your spiritual beliefs and practices are lifelong.
- Maintaining your spiritual practices provides stability amidst the changes of college life.

Benefits of Staying Connected
- **Emotional Support**: Your faith community can offer encouragement and guidance.
- **Moral Compass**: Spiritual practices help you make decisions aligned with your values and avoid making poor choices you may regret later.
- **Community and Fellowship**: Building relationships with like-minded individuals enhances your college experience.

STAYING CONNECTED WITH YOUR HOME FAITH COMMUNITY

Strategies for Staying in Touch

1. Online Services and Sermons
- **Watch Services Online**: Schedule time to view live-streamed or recorded sermons from your home community.
- **Participate Virtually**: Engage in online discussions or virtual small groups.

2. Regular Visits Home
- **Plan Visits**: Aim to attend services or events at your home place of worship when possible.
- **Coordinate with Academic Calendar:** Utilize breaks and holidays to reconnect in person.

3. Communication with Leaders and Members
- **Stay in Contact**: Maintain regular communication through calls, texts, or emails.
- **Share Updates**: Keep your community informed about your experiences and challenges.

DEVELOPING A PLAN FOR SPIRITUAL PRACTICE AT COLLEGE

Finding a Local Faith Community

1. Research Before You Arrive
- **Online Searches:** Look for places of worship near your college.
- **Denominational Directories:** Use official websites to find affiliated communities.

2. Visit Different Communities
- **Attend Services:** Plan to visit a different place each week until you find a good fit.
- **Evaluate Fit:** Consider factors like doctrine, community size, and atmosphere.

3. Connect with Campus Faith Groups
- **Student Organizations:** Explore faith-based clubs or groups on campus.
- **Campus Ministries:** Engage with organizations that cater to college students.

Planning for Personal Devotion and Fellowship

1. Schedule Personal Devotion Time
- **Daily Practices:** Allocate time for prayer, meditation, or reading sacred texts.
- **Consistency:** Establish a routine that fits your academic schedule.

2. Find a Religious Mentor
- **Home Religious Guide:** Continue mentorship remotely.
- **New Faith Leader:** Seek guidance from leaders in your college town.
- **Peer Mentor:** Connect with a fellow student who shares your beliefs.

3. Engage in Fellowship Activities
- **Join Study Groups:** Participate in small group studies or discussions.
- **Volunteer Service:** Get involved in service projects organized by faith communities.

ADDITIONAL IDEAS TO STAY CONNECTED TO YOUR BELIEFS

MAINTAIN ACCOUNTABILITY

Regular Check-Ins
- Schedule a regular, reoccurring time to join in family devotions, even if it must be virtual
- Arrange consistent meetings with your religious mentor

Use Technology
- Utilize apps for prayer reminders, scripture readings, or meditation guides.
- Join forums or social media groups that align with your faith.

EMBRACE NEW OPPORTUNITIES

Interfaith Engagement
- Attend events hosted by different faith groups to broaden understanding.
- Engage in conversations that promote mutual respect and learning.
- Host events with others from outside your faith to increase understanding of your beliefs.

Leadership Roles
- Take initiative and consider leading a faith-based group or organizing events.
- Mentor others to support peers who are also navigating their spiritual journey in college.

OVERCOMING COMMON CHALLENGES

Time Constraints
- Prioritize spiritual activities by scheduling them alongside academic commitments.

Feeling Isolated
- Actively seek out community by attending events and introducing yourself to others.

Cultural differences
- Embrace diversity by learning about different practices and finding common ground, while maintaining a connection to your home faith community to maintain your own beliefs.

SETTING SPIRITUAL GOALS

GOAL-SETTING WORKSHEET

Goal: (e.g., Attend a local place of worship weekly to maintain my spiritual practice)

____

Action Steps: ____

____

____

Potential Challenges and Solutions:

____

____

Goal: (e.g., Join a campus faith group to build a community of like-minded peers)

____

Action Steps: ____

____

____

Potential Challenges and Solutions:

____

____

Goal: (e.g., Schedule daily personal devotion time for reflection and prayer)

____

Action Steps: ____

____

____

Potential Challenges and Solutions:

____

____

SIX-MONTH REFLECTION AND UPDATE

Regular reflection ensures that your spiritual goals remain relevant and achievable.

REFLECTION PROMPTS

Have I maintained my connection with my home faith community? Provide examples.

____

____

How have I integrated into local faith communities or campus groups?

____

____

What challenges have I faced in maintaining my spiritual well-being, and how have I addressed them?

____

____

12-MONTH REFLECTION

Progress summary:

____

____

New insights:

____

____

Goals to add or adjust:

____

____

____

____

Chapter Conclusion

Your spiritual well-being is a vital aspect of your identity. By intentionally planning how to maintain and nurture your faith during this time, you'll create a strong foundation that supports your personal growth, decision-making, and sense of community. Remember, your personal beliefs are a source of strength and guidance. By maintaining your practices, you're not only honoring your values but also enriching your college experience.

STEP 01 — **Develop a Spiritual Plan:** Outline how you'll continue your practices and stay connected.

STEP 02 — **Research and Reach Out:** Identify local communities and campus groups to join.

STEP 03 — **Schedule Activities:** Integrate spiritual practices into your routine.

STEP 04 — **Establish Accountability:** Find mentors or partners to support your journey.

STEP 05 — **Set Reminders for Reflection:** Schedule six-month intervals to review your goals.

EMBRACE THE JOURNEY

College is a transformative time, and nurturing your spiritual well-being will enhance your experience. Stay true to your beliefs, remain open to growth, and let your faith be a source of strength and guidance throughout your college years.

Chapter 12: Maintaining Home Connections in College

Embarking on your college journey is an exciting milestone filled with new experiences, independence, and personal growth. While you may feel thrilled about your newfound freedom, it's natural to also experience homesickness or miss the familiarity of home. Maintaining strong connections with your family and close friends is important for emotional support and can enrich your college experience.

This chapter focuses on setting goals and creating plans to stay connected with your loved ones. We'll explore strategies for scheduling family time, planning for holiday breaks, establishing regular communication, and intentionally keeping in touch with friends who are forging their own paths. By proactively nurturing these relationships, you'll build a supportive network that sustains you throughout your college years and beyond.

THE IMPORTANCE OF STAYING CONNECTED

Emotional Well-being

- **Support System:** Family and close friends provide encouragement, advice, and a listening ear during challenging times.
- **Sense of Belonging:** Staying connected helps maintain a sense of identity and grounding amidst new environments.

Transition for Everyone

- **Family Adjustments:** Remember that your departure is a significant change for your family as well.
- **Mutual Effort:** Regular communication can ease the transition for both you and your loved ones.

STRATEGIES FOR STAYING CONNECTED WITH FAMILY

Schedule Regular Family Time

1. Establish Communication Routines
- **Video Chats:** Schedule weekly or bi-weekly video calls with parents, siblings, or other family members.
- **Phone Calls:** Set a consistent time for phone conversations if video chats aren't feasible.
- **Text Messages:** Send regular updates through texts or messaging apps.

2. Plan for Holiday Breaks and Visits
- **Holiday Planning**: Decide in advance which holidays or breaks you'll spend at home.
- **Coordinate Schedules**: Align your plans with family events or traditions.
- **Book Travel Early**: Arrange transportation ahead of time to save costs and ensure availability.

3. Share Your College Experience
- **Photos and Videos:** Send pictures of your campus, dorm, or events you're attending.
- **Social Media:** Use private groups or accounts to share updates with family members.
- **Letters and Care Packages:** Exchange handwritten letters or small gifts for a personal touch.

ACTION STEPS

Create a communication plan. Include the frequency and preferred method. Set a reminder in you calendar.

____

____

Discuss holiday and visit plans with your family after reviewing your academic calendar. Record planned trips home here. Make the necessary arrangements (e.g., plane tickets).

____

____

____

Discuss shared activities with your family. Is there a show you can all watch and then discuss together? Do you want to have virtual family events or work on collaborative projects during the year? Record your plans here.

____

____

____

MAINTAINING FRIENDSHIPS FROM HOME

Intentional Communication with Friends

1. Schedule Regular Catch-Ups
- **Video Calls:** Plan monthly or bi-weekly virtual hangouts.
- **Group Chats:** Create messaging groups to keep everyone updated and connected.
- **Social Media Engagement:** Share updates, comment on posts, and celebrate each other's achievements.

2. Plan Reunions
- **Holiday Meet-Ups:** Organize gatherings when everyone is back home during breaks.
- **Annual Trips:** Consider planning a yearly trip or retreat together.
- **Attend Events:** Support each other by attending significant events like performances or games when possible.

3. Share Your College Experience
- **Exchange Stories:** Share anecdotes about college life, new friends, and experiences.
- **Collaborate Remotely:** Work on joint projects or hobbies, such as writing, art, or gaming.

ACTION STEPS

Create a friendship maintenance plan. Make a list of friends you want to stay in touch with intentionally, determine how those friends prefer to communicate, then set communication goals (e.g., how often you'll reach out to each friend). Record them here.

____

____

____

You may need to be the first to initiate contact. Don't wait for others to reach out; share your feelings about wanting to stay connected.

Brainstorm activities you can do together. Some ideas include virtual events like game nights, book clubs, or watch parties. Setting mutual goals like fitness challenges or learninga new skill wth regular check-ins can also be fun. Write some ideas that sound fun here.

____

____

____

Distance and differing schedules can make coordination tough; friendships may feel strained or different over time. Reach out with patience and understanding, and be sure to address feelings openly. Focus on quality interactions over quantity.

BALANCING INDEPENDENCE AND HOMESICKNESS

Embracing Independence
- **Explore New Opportunities:** Engage in campus activities to build a sense of belonging.
- **Set Personal Goals:** Focus on your growth and the experiences you want to have.

Coping with Homesickness
- **Acknowledge Your Feelings:** Recognize that missing home is normal and okay.
- **Create a Comfortable Space:** Decorate your living area with familiar items or photos.
- **Establish New Routines:** Build a daily schedule that includes self-care and enjoyable activities.

ACTIONS STEPS

Develop Coping Strategies
- Engage in a mindfulness practice
- Stay active by participating in activities, sports, or clubs

Set Boundaries
- Balance communication - staying in touch is important but allow yourself space to grow independently
- Communicate with family and friends about your availability to avoid becoming overwhelmed

Seek Support
- Utilize campus mental health resources
- Reach out to classmates, roommates, friends, or family

ADDITIONAL TIPS FOR STAYING CONNECTED

Utilize Technology
- **Shared Calendars:** Use apps like Google Calendar to coordinate schedules.
- **Photo Sharing Apps:** Create shared albums to easily exchange photos.
- **Voice Messages:** Send voice notes for a more personal touch when texting.

Be Present During Interactions
- **Active Listening:** Give full attention during conversations, avoiding multitasking.
- **Express Appreciation:** Let your loved ones know you value their support.
- **Share Achievements and Challenges:** Be open about your experiences, fostering deeper connections.

Manage Time Zones and Schedules
- **Flexible Planning:** Be willing to adjust meeting times to accommodate different time zones or busy periods. Recognize when you or your loved ones might be most available.

SIX-MONTH REFLECTION AND UPDATE

Regularly reviewing your efforts to stay connected can help you adjust your approach and maintain healthy relationships.

REFLECTION PROMPTS

Have I maintained regular communication with my family and friends? Provide examples.

____

____

What challenged have I faced in staying connected, and how have I addressed them?

____

____

How have my relationships evolved since starting college?

____

____

Am I experiencing homesickness or difficulties balancing independence and family ties?

____

____

12-MONTH REFLECTION

Progress summary:

____

____

New insights:

____

____

Goals to add or adjust:

____

____

____

Chapter Conclusion

Maintaining strong connections with your family and close friends enriches your college experience and provides a vital support network. By setting intentional goals and creating practical plans to stay in touch, you honor these important relationships while embracing your independence. Remember to communicate regularly by establishing routines, be intentional to stay connected, and adjust your routine as needed.

STEP 01

Establish Communication Plans: Schedule regular calls and visits with family and friends.

STEP 02

Engage in Shared Experiences: Find activities you can enjoy together, even from a distance.

STEP 03

Address Homesickness: Develop coping strategies and seek support when needed. Give yourself time to adjust.

STEP 04

Set Reminders for Reflection: Schedule six-month check-ins to review and adjust your goals.

EMBRACE THE JOURNEY

College is a time of growth, exploration, and new relationships. By staying connected with your roots, you carry the support and love of your family and friends with you, enriching your journey and providing a strong foundation for your future.

Section II Conclusion

As you conclude this second section of the notebook, take a moment to acknowledge the effort and thought you've invested in setting meaningful goals for your college experience. You've explored your personal values, financial aspirations, social ambitions, spiritual practices, and strategies for maintaining strong connections with family and friends. By proactively planning and setting these goals, you're laying a solid foundation for a fulfilling and successful college journey.

THE DYNAMIC NATURE OF GOALS

Remember, the goals you've set are not static. They are meant to evolve as you grow, learn, and encounter new experiences. College is a time of transformation, and it's natural for your priorities and aspirations to shift. By scheduling regular reflections every six months—or when significant changes occur—you ensure that your goals remain aligned with your current self.

CELEBRATE YOUR PROGRESS

As you move forward, celebrate the progress you make, both big and small. Achieving a goal, overcoming a challenge, or simply maintaining consistency in your efforts are all victories worth acknowledging. These accomplishments contribute to your personal growth and confidence.

STAY OPEN AND ADAPTABLE

Stay open to new opportunities and be willing to adjust your goals as needed. Embrace the unexpected, and don't be afraid to explore paths you hadn't initially considered. Your college experience is uniquely yours, and flexibility will allow you to make the most of it.

A SPACE FOR LESSONS LEARNED

As you reach the end of your college journey, it's valuable to look back and consider what you've learned. Use the space below to capture your insights, experiences, and any wisdom you'd like to carry forward.

LESSONS LEARNED

Academic Discoveries: ______________________________

____

Personal Growth: ______________________________

____

Challenges Overcome: ______________________________

____

Unexpected Joys: ______________________________

____

CAPTURING MEMORIES

College is a time filled with memorable moments. Reflect on the experiences that have shaped you, brought you joy, or taught you valuable lessons.

FAVORITE MEMORIES

An Unforgettable Event: ______________________________

____

A Meaningful Friendship: ______________________________

____

A Proud Achievement: ______________________________

____

A Moment of Growth: ______________________________

____

ADVICE FOR FUTURE COLLEGE STUDENTS

Your experiences can offer guidance to those who will follow in your footsteps. Consider what advice you would give to future college students embarking on their own journeys.

WORDS OF WISDOM

on Choosing a College: _______________________________

____

On Setting Goals: _______________________________

____

On Overcoming Challenges: _______________________________

____

On Making the Most of College Life: _______________________________

____

REFLECTING ON WHAT YOU MIGHT HAVE DONE DIFFERENTLY

Hindsight can provide valuable insights. Reflecting on what you might have done differently doesn't diminish your achievements; it enhances your understanding and growth.

REFLECTIONS

Different Approaches to Challenges: _______________________________

____

Opportunities Not Pursued: _______________________________

____

Habits You Would Change: _______________________________

____

Lessons for Future Endeavors: _______________________________

____

Final Thoughts

Your college journey is a unique tapestry woven from your experiences, choices, challenges, and triumphs. This notebook has been a tool to help you navigate that journey with intention and self-awareness.

EMBRACE LIFELONG LEARNING

As you step into the next chapter of your life, carry forward the habit of setting goals, reflecting on your experiences, and adapting to change. Lifelong learning and personal growth don't end with college; they continue throughout your life.

CELEBRATE YOUR ACHIEVEMENTS

Take pride in what you've accomplished. Every step you've taken has contributed to who you are today. Acknowledge your hard work, resilience, and dedication.

STAY CONNECTED

Maintain the relationships and connections you've built during this time. They are part of your support system and can enrich your life in countless ways.

LOOK FORWARD WITH CONFIDENCE

You are equipped with the tools, insights, and experiences to face future challenges and opportunities. Trust in your abilities, stay true to your values, and continue to pursue your passions.

THANK YOU FOR ALLOWING THIS NOTEBOOK TO BE PART OF YOUR JOURNEY

May it serve as a cherished record of your growth and a reminder of your strength and potential. Wishing you all the best in your future endeavors.

EMBRACE THE JOURNEY

Trust that you have the tools and self-awareness to make the choice that's right for you. Whatever decision you make, it's the beginning of an exciting new chapter in your life.

Additional Resources

Here are some websites and organizations that are great resources as you prepare for college.

COLLEGE VISIT PLANNING

- **Preview Days**: Check for special events held at colleges you're interested in. Future student events are a great way to see campus and meet key college staff.

COLLEGE PREP

If you need to show college readiness due to less than stellar grades, or just want to get a head start on your college credits, here are some great resources:

- **CLEP**: Exams that some colleges accept passing scores as college credit. Be sure to check with specific colleges to see which CLEP exams they accept (www.clep.collegeboard.org)
  - CLEP exams have a fee but students may be able to obtain waivers through their school or by completing free prep classes through Modern States (www.modernstates.org)
- **Running Start**: Check for local colleges or through your high school for running start programs that allow you to take low cost or free college courses
- **College in the High School**: Some high schools teach college courses through CIH. Be sure to check with your counselors and follow instructions to receive college credit.

FINANCIAL AID AND SCHOLARSHIP INFORMATION

- **Federal Student Aid:** Includes resources to learn more about grants and loans; also has FAFSA applications and information (www.studentaid.gov)
- **Finaid**: This site has a ton of financial aid information and tools for estimated federal aid or calculating future loan payments (www.finaid.org)
- **College Board**: BigFuture is College Board's scholarship search (www.bigfuture.collegeboard.org)
- **Scholarship360**: Matches students to scholarships and also has options based on "easy to apply for" and "no essay" scholarships (www.scholarship360.org)
- **FastWeb**: A scholarship database to search through, or create a profile and the database will match scholarships for you (www.fastweb.com)
- **High School Counselors**: Use this resource for local scholarship opportunities

Note: websites and resources may change over time. These resources were available November 2024.

Additional Resources

Here are some websites and organizations that are great resources as you prepare for college.

COMPARING COLLEGES

- **College Scorecard**: College comparison tool provided by the U.S. Dept. of Education. This tool allows comparison between colleges, costs, and fields of study (www.collegescorecard.ed.gov)
    - It's important to note the debt comparison *only includes federal loans*; schools that exceed federal loan limits and require private loans may seem misrepresented
- **College Board**: College Board's BigFuture site includes a college search as well as a career search option (www.bigfuture.collegeboard.org)
- **U.S. News and World Report**: Signing up for a free account allows students to search through ranked colleges (www.usnews.com/best-colleges/compare)
- **Niche**: This site offers easy comparisons between colleges and also includes reviews and ratings from current or past students (www.niche.com)

INFORMATION FOR PARENTS

- **Same as students!**: Many of the resources listed for students have related sites for parents.
- **College Newsletters**: Check at specific colleges for newsletters aimed at parents and families.
- **Grown and Flown Blog**: This blog has been extremely helpful to me as a parent. With staff and guest writers covering helpful tips, funny anecdotes, and the ups and downs of the changing roles as children become young adults, this blog has something for everyone with children from middle school to college age (www.grownandflown.com)

Note: websites and resources may change over time. These resources were available November 2024.

LARGER TABLES FROM EARLIER CHAPTERS

The next few pages hold larger versions of the tables included in this guide. The larger tables may be easier to fill out if you need to include a lot of information. For some tables, it may be useful to make copies before filling them out so you can add more colleges, share with friends, or update the information as you learn more.

Fillable Cost Estimate Table - From Page 8

College Name	Tuition & Fees	Room & Board	Books & Supplies	Other Expenses	Estimated Total Cost

TIPS FOR FILLING OUT TABLES

- **Tuition & Fees:** Check the college's official website for the most recent figures.
- **Room & Board:** Consider on-campus vs. off-campus housing costs.
- **Other Expenses:** Include transportation, personal expenses, and health insurance.

Fillable Cost Estimate Table - From Page 9

College Name	Tuition & Fees	Room & Board	Books & Supplies	Other Expenses	Scholarships & Grants	Loans Offered	Net Cost

Scholarship Tracking Table - From Page 11

Scholarship Name	Provider	Amount	Requirements	Deadline	Application Status
					Not Started / In Progress / Submitted!
					Not Started / In Progress / Submitted!
					Not Started / In Progress / Submitted!
					Not Started / In Progress / Submitted!

Social and Housing Priorities Tables - From Pages 27 and 34

RANKING YOUR SOCIAL PRIORITIES

Use the table below to rank your social interests from most to least important.

Priority Rank	Social Aspect	Notes

RANKING YOUR HOUSING PREFERENCE

Use the table below to rank what's most important to you regarding housing.

Priority Rank	Housing Aspect	Notes

Admission Requirements Tracking Table - From Page 40

Use the table below to record key admissions information for each college.

College Name	Courses Required	Min. GPA	Average GPA	Test Required (SAT/ACT)	Average Test Scores	Acceptance Rate	Additional Requirements

Admission Requirements Tracking Table - From Page 51

College Name	Financial Fit	Academics	Social Scene	Housing	Admissions Fit	Campus Feel	Total Score

1. **Define a Scoring Scale:** Use a consistent scale for all categories (e.g., 1 to 5, where 5 is the highest satisfaction).

2. **Evaluate Each Category:** For each college, rate the financial fit, available academic programs and majors, social scene, housing options, admissions alignment, and your impression of the campus.

3. **Calculate Total Scores:** Sum the points for each college to get a total score.

Embrace
Your
Journey